Minnesota

by Joan Claire Graham & 37 Friends

Before movies, radio, television and the Internet, people spent millenniums perfecting the art of storytelling. The world's oldest form of entertainment owes its longevity to its simplicity and to the timeless appeal of a well-told story. Unlike news reporters who hit readers in the first paragraph with all they really need to know, a storyteller unfolds events like a screenplay with an establishing shot, story exposition, ascending action, conflict, climax and resolution.

As I travel around Minnesota, talking to people and inviting them to send me their best true stories to share with the world in the *Minnesota Memories* book series, I am always impressed by their knowledge, their instinctive need to share what they know, and their innate ability to choose a storytelling style that will evoke a response from their intended audience, whether that response is laughter, understanding, sympathy, empathy, nostalgia, or amazement at unusual things that really happen.

Hollywood screenwriters have spent thousands of highly-paid hours inventing some crazy Minnesota stories and characters. Rose of *The Golden Girls* was the stupid one, Jerry Lundegaard in *Fargo* was a bungling crook, and Ted Baxter in *The Mary Tyler Moore Show* demonstrated how inept a newsman could be—if he was broadcasting from Minneapolis. When I moved away to other states and told people I was from Minnesota, they looked sympathetic and started talking slower. Convincing them to ignore those media-made stereotypes and believe that Minnesota people are actually intelligent, hard-working, good-humored, highly educated, creative and resourceful people was difficult.

So I decided to give genuine Minnesota people, who do such a good job of storytelling, a chance to show the world what we're *really* like by writing and publishing their own true stories. These are not Ole and Lena jokes, nor do they contain hot dish lore or the phrase "you betcha." *Minnesota Memories* are real stories by real Minnesota people, and reading them is just a lot more fun than a person ought to be able to have. If this is your first *Minnesota Memories* volume, welcome aboard, and if you like this book, check out the five that preceded it.

Joan Claire Graham, Purveyor of Memories

Cover by Aquinata "Cookie" Graham. Thanks, Mom!

Back cover photo: Leah Nell Peterson, Cannon Falls Beacon

Special thanks to Sara Aeikens, story wrangler

ISBN: 0971 1971 56

Table of Contents

Table of Contents

Mix Master Madness
by Joan Claire Graham

After saving, swapping, sorting, sticking and counting for several years, my mother packed all her Green Stamp books in a shoe box and went downtown to the redemption center to claim her prize--a multi-speed Sunbeam Mix Master.

I don't know why she wanted that mixer because Mother didn't do well with mechanical things, and she was not much of a cook. The only dessert we had on a regular basis was chocolate cake, made from a Betty Crocker mix. Prior to getting her Mix Master, we'd managed just fine by mixing ingredients in a brown earthenware bowl, counting strokes as we stirred with a spoon. I'm sure that's how I learned to count because I always got into the act. Licking chocolate cake batter from the bowl and spoon was my favorite part of the process. Mother's new mixer took up more cupboard space than the old spoon and bowl, but she thought it was modern, and I didn't mind licking batter off two beaters in addition to a mixing bowl and new rubber spoon.

Usually we didn't bother to frost our chocolate cake because we all preferred to smear butter on it. After I was 12 years old, I would typically take on the responsibility of making a cake on Saturday morning, and there was never a crumb left by Sunday. All afternoon and evening we'd take turns stealing out to the kitchen, cutting a piece, buttering and eating it. Warm chocolate cake with butter was the best, but even the last cold crumbs scraped off the bottom of the cake pan were good enough to satisfy my sweet tooth.

One Saturday morning when I was in junior high, Mom's new Mix Master got me into big trouble. Even worse than that, we had to do without our chocolate cake that week.

The Mix Master had a grooved revolving turntable, and the bowls that came with the mixer had bottoms designed to fit onto those grooves. As the motor started, the bowls revolved, and the speed of rotation correlated with the speed of the beaters. I'm not sure I understand the advantage of this feature, but I think Sunbeam still makes Mix Masters with rotating turntables.

I was in a hurry to get my chocolate cake into the oven, so I turned the mixer up to its highest speed. Just at that moment the telephone in the kitchen rang, so I walked away from my project to answer it. When I looked back over my shoulder from the phone, I was shocked and horrified. In the thirty seconds it took to turn my back and answer the phone, the centrifugal force in the rapidly spinning Mix Master bowl had caused the cake batter to crawl up its inside wall. As the stuff reached the top, the continued circular motion from the rapidly rotating turntable flung the batter around the kitchen in a chocolate cyclone.

I slammed down the receiver and dodged the onslaught of flying batter as I fought my way to the counter, reached into the vortex of a chocolate swirling shower and turned off the mixer. The kitchen looked like a chocolate crime scene as splashes of batter dripped from cupboards, walls, windows, me and the ceiling. Gravity being what it is, the size of the mess just kept growing as batter dribbled and oozed down from high places. Just as I was trying to figure out how to clean up this gigantic mess without incurring the wrath of my mother, my uncle Johnny walked in the back door, assessed the situation, and started laughing so hard he could hardly stand up.

My uncle was the only person who found this incident funny that day, as there were several negative consequences. For one, Mother was hopping mad. Why had I turned the mixer up to high speed? Why hadn't I turned it off before I answered the phone? Didn't I have the brains I was born with? Those were hard questions to answer in my state of surprise and embarrassment as my uncle continued to laugh at my feisty mother, his splattered niece and our chocolate spin-art kitchen.

It took at least an hour to clean up the mess. The wooden cupboards, formica counter top, tile floor, stainless steel sink, glass windows and metal appliances cleaned up great. It wasn't easy though. We used rags and sponges, and the greasy, colorful batter had to be rinsed out constantly. Every time I thought I had finished the job, I'd find another glob clinging to an obscure cranny, and the batter got harder to remove as it dried.

I was due for my Saturday bath and hair washing anyway, and I cleaned up pretty well too. But many chocolate stalactites had dangled for a few minutes from our kitchen ceiling, and the plaster or sheet rock up there never fully recovered. Even after I stood on the counter and scrubbed with a sponge and Spic 'n Span several times, we could still see residual chocolate grease spots. Over the next several weeks or months we even painted the ceiling a couple of times, but after awhile the cake batter grease spots would bleed through the paint.

I eventually saw the humor and told this story many times over the years--often pointing out those cake batter spots to incredulous relatives and friends. When I cleaned out that house prior to its sale in 1993, I showed the stains to my daughter. Two years ago, when the house was again for sale, I attended an open house and was not surprised to see that the evidence from my 1960 Mix Master mishap was still slightly visible on the kitchen ceiling. I have no idea what kind of high-impact, insoluble oil Betty Crocker put into her chocolate cake mixes back in those days, but whatever it was, Betty's batter left indelible marks on that kitchen ceiling and on my memory.

The Sunbeam Mix Master
with revolving turntable

The Railroads Run Through the Middle of the Town
by Joan Claire Graham

On Tuesday nights I attend a writers' group at the home of Love Cruikshank, who provides inspiration for us because she continues to write for the *Albert Lea Tribune* as she approaches her tenth decade of life. We sit in a circle and take turns reading pieces we've written, and whoever sits in the fourth seat has a good chance of being interrupted or drowned out as the 7:30 train comes roaring by, about fifty yards from her house. First comes the whistle and then the rumble and vibration produced by the energy of all those tons of rolling steel.

That old Rosemary Clooney song, "The Railroad Comes Through the Middle of the House," starts going through my head as the interrupted reader pauses to wait until the house stops shaking. Love usually shrugs and says, "You know, I don't even hear those trains anymore. I've grown so used to ignoring them over the years."

I usually ignore trains too, because there are fewer of them now, but I can remember when they played a huge role in my daily life. Albert Lea's railroad history goes back to the Victorian era. The Illinois Central ran from Baton Rouge to Albert Lea by the late 1800s, and the Rock Island connected Albert Lea to St. Louis in 1902.

Throughout the years, Albert Lea was serviced by at least a half dozen railroads, and rail accessibility contributed to the early success of Wilson's and other industries that helped build the town. Three depots stand as proof that passenger trains took people wherever they wanted to go long before automobiles and airplanes took over that job. Trains also hauled mail, grain and fresh milk to and from every little community.

My family knew at least two guys who worked as train engineers, and boys of my generation admired these men. Most railroad employees lived in town, but itinerant inspectors and maintenance workers stayed temporarily at rooming houses or the Allis Hotel and ate at local cafes. Their dark blue and white striped Lee overalls and caps identified them as rail workers.

Our house on First Avenue was built in the early 1900s, just a block west of the tracks. Hundreds of houses like ours were built and furnished with materials shipped by rail from large cities. Manufactured goods, farm products, and livestock rode to and from Albert Lea by rail.

Three rail lines ran through Albert Lea when I was a kid. I loved the Rock Island depot near the packinghouse because going there meant I was either taking a trip to the Twin Cities or meeting someone coming in on the train. When we wanted to see Dayton's, Donaldson's and Powers' Christmas decorations in Minneapolis, my mom and I would wait on the platform for the Rocket to come roaring in from the south, and as I stood there, the blast of energy, sound and wind from the train nearly knocked me off my feet.

Trains were both a blessing and a curse when I was a kid. Although we appreciated the link to faraway places, we complained about the noise day and night and especially about the inconvenience whenever a stopped freight train blocked our way.

The Minneapolis and St. Louis tracks near my house carried mostly freight trains. A few blocks southeast, under the viaduct, there was an extensive train yard, where switchmen unhitched incoming freight cars and hitched up cars containing outgoing loads. A roundhouse contained a turntable for engines, and that switching yard was a busy place.

We could predict the length of a train by counting the number of diesel engines. Four engines meant a hundred or maybe two hundred cars. Freight trains traveling north were likely to pass our residential crossings in a few minutes as their engines picked up speed outside town. But trains going south into our switching yard almost always stopped and created a roadblock that could last from a few minutes to an hour or more. Unlike Germans, Albert Lea natives could not set their clocks by the arrival of their trains, so we were often caught on the wrong side of the tracks.

With three rail lines crisscrossing town, going anywhere involved crossing tracks. To go to school or downtown, I had to cross tracks on Water Street. If I wanted to go to Abbot Field to fly kites or see a football game, I had to cross tracks at Summer Avenue. To go to Morin Park, I had to cross tracks on Clark Street--unless I walked across the viaduct on Main Street. Our viaduct willingly lifted any pedestrian or motorist over the top of the switching yard and any stopped trains, but the traveler had to be willing or able to go a few extra blocks--an additional ten minutes by foot and an extra minute by car.

My grade school and high school were just a few blocks from my home--both quick and easy walks unless the morning train was off schedule, which happened every now and then. School administrators refused to accept being stuck behind a train as an excuse for tardiness. We were expected to either back up and hike across the viaduct or wait for the train to clear the crossing. Either way, we'd be tardy. I don't even know if they still use the word "tardy" in schools, but tardiness demerits posed a threat to a good school record by showing prospective employers and college admissions people how irresponsible and undependable you were. I don't know if that was actually true, but we bought it, and that's why we risked our lives.

It was impossible to predict that any train that had sped into town would stop for a long time and block our way. Since the term, "get a ride to school over the viaduct" had not been invented by anybody's parents, we kids who got stuck on the wrong side of the train had to resort to risking our lives in order to avoid school disciplinary measures. I ran across tracks several times while a whistling train was bearing down, and I crawled under and over stopped trains several times.

Crawling over the hitch was scary because when the train started, parts of the hitch would tighten. The prospect of getting a foot caught was realistic and terrifying. While wearing a dress and a few can can slips, hoisting myself up there and jumping down without flashing my underwear was a real challenge. The train started one time while I was climbing over the hitch, but I managed to parachute down to the other side before it picked up any speed.

Crawling under the train was equally terrifying because sometimes the train would roll back while cars were being hitched or unhitched in the rail yard. Before crawling under, we'd go to the middle of the boxcar so we'd have a few seconds to get out of the way of the wheels if the car moved backward or forward, then we'd check for things hanging down that might snag us or our clothes. Whether we climbed over or crawled under, we'd go to the hitch first and toss our books and bags over to the other side. It was dangerous activity, and since my mother would have had a fit if she had found out about it, I had the good sense not to tell her.

Getting crushed by a freight train was a very real possibility. All of us children from St. Theodore's assembled in church one day and watched pall bearers sadly carry in a little white coffin containing the body of our school mate Jimmy Joe Donohue, who had been killed by a train as he played on the tracks down behind the feed store.

From time to time newspaper headlines announced the train-related death of a pedestrian, driver, or car full of people. We were supposed to watch out for our own safety, and very few crossings in those days had gates or warning lights. It's easy to understand how distracted, tired or inebriated drivers failed to see or hear an oncoming train.

Clark Street, just north of the switching yard, had a crossing bar that closed to block off several pairs of tracks that sliced through that street. When I was little, this crossing was staffed by a railroad worker in a shack. The shack, which was about seven feet long and five feet wide, was equipped with a stove, a long, padded leather bench, a retractable table, and radio communication equipment.

One guard in the Clark Street shack had lost an arm in a switching accident, and he liked to visit with kids who stopped by to chat or play cards. His job was to listen for a radio message so he could let down the gate manually and hang a lantern on it whenever a train passed. Eventually the shack, the gate and the man were replaced by electronic equipment.

Getting caught behind a train was usually not troublesome when we were heading for home, with no tardy bells or starting time to worry about. We'd patiently wait it out, enjoying the extra time to talk with friends, counting boxcars or noting all railroad lines that had cars running on this particular train. One favorite trick was to stand in one place and stare at one spot on the moving train, which created the sensation that the train was standing still and we were moving.

Annoying homeward trips occurred on Sunday mornings. Even though a very long inbound freight train crossed the intersection at Fountain and Vine a little before or a little after 10 a.m. every Sunday, and despite the fact that it invariably drove into the switching yard three blocks south of this point and stopped for a long time, and despite the fact that we got stuck behind a stopped train at least once a month as we drove home from church--and despite the fact that-- on his insistence--we were highly trained to streamline our homeward trip by sprinting down the church steps, hopping into the car and screeching away from the curb so that we'd be the first Catholics home after 9 o'clock mass, despite all these things--Dad refused to alter his route home and drive an extra four blocks over the viaduct.

Why did he refuse to drive those extra four blocks? Because if there was no train stopped on the tracks, he would save forty-five seconds to a minute. Time after time, once he realized he was stuck behind yet another train, he'd cuss and groan and threaten to call the railroad, the police, or the city manager. But would he back the car up, turn around and go over the viaduct? No, because the extra distance was too far out of his way, and he feared that by the time he drove "all the way around," the train would have already cleared the crossing.

We sometimes sat there for a half hour or longer--cold in winter and hot in summer. My brother would complain that he had to go to the bathroom, my mother would worry about getting our traditional Sunday midday roast into the oven on time, and I'd be bored out of my mind and unwilling to bring up the subject of turning around and using the viaduct for fear of getting yelled at. By the time the little red caboose showed up, we were all in a mutinous state. In eighteen years I probably spent six months of quality family time stuck on the other side of trains because my dad refused to drive over the viaduct. God prevent my head from ever becoming that thick!

Another interesting social phenomenon we experienced by living near the tracks was sharing a small part of our lives with occasional bums or hobos, mostly men, who rode the rails. Some railroad workers chased them away, but others tolerated them or even helped them find empty boxcars because they brought helpful information about the line into the yards. Some traveled in boxcars, some rode on the tops, and others rode under the train. Some cars were built with rods underneath to stabilize and keep them from swaying, and a few very resourceful hobos took grain doors and laid them suspended across the rods, and crawled up onto the doors, where they rode at high speeds while lying two feet off the ground. They often wrapped themselves in cardboard or paper to stay warm, but railroad workers occasionally found hobos frozen to death under the train, in refrigerator cars or mutilated with hands and arms pinched in doors.

Albert Lea had a little shanty town hobo encampment near the tracks, not far from the viaduct. My brother took me there once, and I remember seeing traces of civilization-- bean cans with jagged cut-off tops, bonfire remnants, cardboard boxes, discarded clothes, scattered playing cards, and girlie magazines--all the necessities of life.

Once in awhile a hobo would knock on our back door and politely ask my mother for food, and she always gave him something. Feeding the hungry was the decent thing to do, but she was also slightly afraid that this mysterious stranger--or his friends--might come back for revenge if she turned him away.

When trucks, planes and cars started hauling people, mail, milk, livestock and merchandise conveniently and cheaply, railroads started to experience hard times. When the many trains that used to pass through Albert Lea each day dwindled to a mere trickle, and when fewer of those trains bothered to stop or even slow down, the depots closed, and switching yard activity nearly stopped. Last spring, as I walked through the old switching yard, I was shocked to see so many rusty and abandoned rails scattered in a place that used to be a beehive of activity.

A few freight trains still pass through Albert Lea every day, many carrying tons of coal or potash in identical open-top box cars, but they rarely stop--thus eliminating the need for school kids to risk their lives crawling over or under them. The packing house where trains used to stop is now a pile of rubble, and little hotels and restaurants that used to serve railroad workers have either closed or found new clientele.

The U.S. Postal Service seems to be doing just fine with trucks, and dairy farmers who used to count on trains to get their product to market before it spoiled have sold out to factory farmers. Most crossings now have electric warning signs or stop signs, and some have been closed off to auto traffic, so we hear of fewer train accidents involving pedestrians or cars these days.

I no longer experience either the convenience of riding trains to faraway places or the annoyance of getting stuck on the wrong side of a standing freight, but the railroads are still a small part of my life. In the night, half awake, I still hear train whistles as freights rumble through town. Sometimes I drive my car parallel to a freight train crossing the great prairies of Minnesota. And I definitely experience the power of the iron horse at 7:30 every Tuesday night just when the fourth reader gets to the best part her story at Love Cruikshank's house.

The rail yard near the Milwaukee Road depot in Albert Lea

Crime and Punishment
by Joan Claire Graham

Like most kids, I loved the taste of hot, charred, squishy marshmallows that we toasted at the end of every picnic. The worst offense I ever committed as a child, however, was standing in the wrong place while my dad did the toasting.

We were enjoying a family picnic at Edgewater Park in Albert Lea when I was 4 years old, and by the time the sun started sinking in the west, thc only thing keeping mosquitoes from devouring us was the smoke from our campfire. We kids had spent the afternoon chasing each other in games of tag, playing on Edgewater's huge slide, and pumping the swings so high we felt we were flying. My long curls, the object of personal vanity and public admiration, stuck to my head in the evening heat. It was time to go home, and we were almost ready. We had done all there was to do--except toast marshmallows.

The fire from roasting hot dogs had diminished to glowing embers, and there were plenty of marshmallows. My brother and I searched for good roasting sticks and spent time peeling their bark and breaking off extra little twigs that might get in the way. An ideal stick was about three feet long and forked at the end, allowing Dad to put two marshmallows on each prong and toast more treats per minute.

After devouring several gooey treats, I stood a respectable distance from my dad while I waited for more. As he pulled a stick with a flaming marshmallow out of the embers and shook it to extinguish the fire, the blazing glob of goo became airborne, flew about six feet and landed on my neck. I let out a scream, and the party came to an abrupt halt as everyone tried to find cold water to soothe my burn.

The scene eventually calmed down, but there was a lot of adult conversation in the car on the way home about how it was a good thing the marshmallow hadn't started my hair on fire. With a fresh burn on my neck, I didn't feel all that lucky, but they made a case for how the whole incident could have been a lot worse.

As I nursed my wound in the back seat, my dad made a suggestion that seemed to make sense to my mom. "The next time she might not be so lucky. Why don't you take her to the barber and have all that hair cut off?" I was afraid she just might do that, so I cried and begged and said I was sorry for standing in the wrong place.

But my pleas fell on deaf ears. The next day Mom took me, kicking and screaming, to get all my hair cut off. Not only did I lose my pretty curls, but I had to have it done at Ray's Barbershop, a men's place that smelled like Butch Wax and Bay Rum cologne.

Ray didn't get many 4-year-old girl customers so he did what he knew best; he cut my hair short--like a boy's. It was too short to curl so I lost my admirable feminine asset. I hated looking like a boy so much that I spent a significant part of the summer of 1950 in silence. I refused to talk.

While I suffered in silence, my parents told anyone who would listen the story about my narrow escape from burning to death after getting hit with a flaming marshmallow--reiterating how lucky we all were that my hair hadn't gone up in flames, and always adding their sage epilogue, "The next day we took her to the barber and had all her curls cut off."

I've heard that the difference between guilt and shame is that the individual feels guilty after doing something wrong. She feels shame, however, when an audience witnesses or hears about the wrongdoing and expresses negative interest.

There I was with a burn on my little neck and chopped-off hair--feeling ashamed for being in the wrong place at a picnic. I never heard anybody defend me or ask my dad, "Don't you think it was the adult who was responsible? Couldn't you just kick yourself for being so careless?"

With a little scar to remind me of that incident, I continued to feel guilty and ashamed until I grew up. After I realized how unjustly I had been punished for my dad's mistake, I used to joke that it would have been more appropriate for my dad to have had his arm cut off. That would have definitely saved me from future flaming marshmallow projectile peril.

But my dad never admitted fault, and my hair stayed short. My parents continued to wage war against my long hair for as long as I lived at home, but when the flower children of the late '60s introduced long hair, I was out in the world, on my own. I let my grow and kept it long until I was 40 years old, but unfortunately, by that time my curls had gone away permanently. When I had little girls of my own, I was able to vicariously experience the joy of curls. We never experienced a near-miss with a marshmallow, and they didn't have to cut their hair off until they felt like doing so.

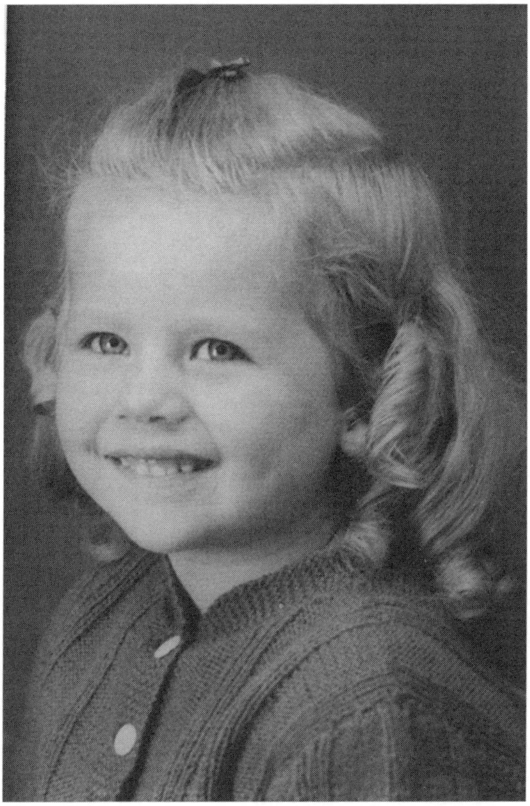

Me and my curls, before the picnic

Skeeter
by Joan Claire Graham

Last year I sent my mother-in-law a copy of *A Pictorial History of Freeborn County, Volume 2.* While leafing through the book, she stopped on page 43. There was a picture of the 1942 Albert Lea Tigers Basketball team, and there stood Skeeter Ochs. Upon seeing the photo, Betty relayed a story I had never heard before.

She told me that when she was a kid, her family lived on a farm a mile and a half south of town. They had six kids--three boys and three girls. While the men were out in the fields with machinery harvesting or threshing, kids from town would sometimes ride their bikes out and watch. After the noon meal, they would happily clean up any leftover food. One particular kid befriended her family. At first he would go home when the other kids left, but then he started to stay over. It was Depression times, and he came from a family with ten kids. Like many at that time, they were going through tough times, so Betty's folks agreed to let Skeeter stay with them.

Irvin and Jo Wayne, Betty's parents, treated Skeeter like one of the family, and he pitched in to help with chores. He was three years younger than Betty was, closer to her brother Bob's age. After he graduated from Albert Lea High School in 1942, Skeeter enlisted in the Navy. Betty's older brother Richard enlisted too, so her mother wrote letters to both boys while they were fighting in World War II. Richard was a gunner on a B-24, and Skeeter entered officer training and became an ensign in 1944. In 1945 he became a lieutenant.

Betty's brother Richard was shot down and killed in the Pacific Theater in 1943, but Skeeter served four years as a hellcat pilot flying missions off the carriers *Enterprise* and *Hancock.* When he made it back to Albert Lea in August of 1946, the Waynes were among those who were happy to see him again.

To maintain his flying skills after the war, Skeeter enlisted in the Naval Reserve at Wold Chamberlain Field in Minneapolis. In the summer of 1947, he was called for training flights. Betty's dad was out in the field one day when Skeeter flew in low in his Navy plane, pulled up and went on his way. "He just wanted to show Mom and Dad how he could fly. I had married and moved away by then, but when they told me about it, I said I didn't think Skeeter should be doing that," she said.

On July 2, Betty's dad and a neighbor were working with a hay loader when a plane approached from the south. It was Skeeter again. After circling the area at a very low altitude, he pulled up to move on his way north, but one of the wings of his plane caught the oak tree in front of the Wayne house. Immediately the plane started to fall apart, dropping pieces across the field. When the engine and fuselage came down, Skeeter was instantly killed. Someone covered his body with his partially opened parachute.

Because of the noise of the low-flying plane, several people looked up from what they had been doing and watched this horrible tragedy, including some neighbor kids who were having a party. One of the first on the scene was Betty's little brother Tommy, who was playing in the yard with his 7-year-old friends. People in town flocked to see this wreck, creating a traffic jam on an otherwise quiet country road.

The local newspaper printed extensive coverage of the crash the next day in a huge article that included the basic news story, photographs and interviews. A commandant for the Navy investigated the incident and issued a statement, condemning the practice of "flat hatting," a Navy term for showing off by flying low. Shocked and grieving family and friends would have preferred sympathy to censure in the aftermath of this tragedy. Skeeter was a local boy who served his country admirably. He became an officer despite his youth and lack of experience.

He may have been acting recklessly that day, but he was a good kid who would probably have done pretty well in life. It was ironic that after surviving combat missions in the war he died in the front yard of the house where he had grown up. He was only 23 years old.

Keith "Skeeter" Ochs

The Theater on Vineland Place
by Joan Claire Graham

Sir Tyrone Guthrie's name did not ring a bell in the early '60s. My friends and I grew up in Albert Lea, and our theater background consisted of school plays, Sunday school pageants and maybe a production of *Deadwood Dick* in the Black Hills. Those with older siblings may have seen college productions, and occasionally someone would come back from Minneapolis and tell us about attending a play at the University of Minnesota Showboat or maybe even a star-studded road show of a musical comedy, but we were essentially culturally illiterate. We honestly didn't know the difference between professional theater and a class play in which a 16-year-old kid with white shoe polish in his hair had a go at playing Willy Loman.

Twin Cities Sunday newspapers reported that Guthrie was coming to town looking for a place to build a professional repertory theater. Then came news that Minneapolis had been chosen over seven other cities, including San Francisco, Chicago and Cleveland. Time passed, and then one day in September of 1962 I saw a picture in the *Minneapolis Tribune*. Tyrone Guthrie towered there like Atlas in a raincoat amidst what he wanted to assure us was soon to become his beautiful new theater on Vineland Place. He stood in front of the wooden skeleton of his thrust stage amidst beams, sub structure, standing water and hanging work lights, and it looked like such a mess I couldn't imagine it would be ready to go in a few months. I still didn't understand why everyone was making a big fuss about it.

During the spring of my junior year, my humanities teacher, Wally Kennedy, did not even try to contain his excitement about the premiere season of the Guthrie Theater. Only a few days after opening night in May, 1963, our class rode a bus to Minneapolis to see a matinee performance of *Hamlet*, directed by Sir Tyrone himself and starring George Grizzard, Jessica Tandy and Hume Cronyn. We kids really didn't know who those actors were, we didn't understand the historical significance of attending that premiere production, and we didn't realize that our lives would be permanently affected by having a theater of this caliber a relatively short distance from where we lived.

From the minute our bus pulled into the muddy area in front of the theatre, I knew it was going to be an adventure. A cutaway concrete facade decorated the outside, and inside we admired the asymmetrical thrust stage, the irregular-shaped 1400-seat auditorium and the multicolored seats. Like the kids that we were, we fussed over what color seat everyone was sitting in.

Costumed heralding trumpeters played a fanfare written especially for the Guthrie, calling patrons to their seats at the beginning of each act, and I still remember the tune. Our seats that day were high off stage left, in the last rows of the section later dubbed the Alps. Although we were no farther than 45 feet from the stage, I had a hard time hearing some of the actors, but I enjoyed the experience and hoped to return.

My wish came true on April 23, 1964, when Orv Gilmore took his senior humanities kids to a double header that featured Shaw's *St. Joan* in the afternoon and Shakespeare's *Henry V* at night. Gilmore referred to the plays as *Hank 5* and *Joanie,* and anticipation of our big day in Minneapolis put us in a springtime celebratory mood.

Since our field trip coincided with Shakespeare's 400th birthday, we kids organized candles and cupcakes and held a birthday party in Loring Park between shows. While 400 candles blazed and our voices sang out to the bard, a Minneapolis Tribune photographer snapped a photo that I still have in my scrapbook.

After building his theater, Tyrone Guthrie, a practical as well as artistic visionary, tackled the early challenge of building an audience for his theater. While directing plays and trying to convey his vision for the artistic direction during the first three seasons, he also addressed acoustical problems and worked to train actors to speak with the intention of being heard and understood, and he enlisted the help of engineers until eventually the building's acoustics were fine tuned to perfection.

Guthrie realized the importance of establishing a base of future patrons and offered low cost student tickets, and throughout college I saved pennies to attend plays. A half hour before curtain time, all available tickets were sold for just a couple of dollars, and by the time I saw *The Cherry Orchard* and *The Way of the World* in 1965, I had come to fully understand and appreciate what a class act I was privileged to witness at the Guthrie Theater. Actors, designers and directors who were respected throughout the world helped educate and convert me to full-fledged theater fan.

More than three hundred plays and countless concerts have been staged at the Guthrie Theater on Vineland Place, and I attended dozens of them over a span of nearly a half century. If I were a theater critic or historian, I might be able to recall a little something scholarly or pretentious about most of them. My most precious memories of the theater on Vineland Place, however, are of personal and family experiences, benchmarks of my life and emotional and unique moments held dear by three generations of family and friends who shared my good times there. I took my little sister to see *Merton of the Movie*s and *The Tempest* when she was a kid. She got hooked, and when she married and moved to Oregon, she raised theater kids.

In 1970 I attended a Summer Arts Study Workshop for teachers in northern Minnesota, and our instructor was Michael Langham, the Guthrie's new artistic director. Meeting and learning from the director gave me a deeper connection and made me feel responsible for finding a way to share the Guthrie experience with the kids I taught. Logistics were tricky, and some kids responded better than others, but it was always worthwhile. After I took a group of students to see *Room Service* in '83, they asked me to take them to see *Master Harold and the Boys* the next year.

A few weeks after the birth of my first daughter in 1975, I hired my first baby sitter so I could escape to a Guthrie matinee, where I could relax and collect my wits for three quiet, colic-free hours. My husband and I spent an entire Sunday following the epic odyssey of *Peer Gynt*, and during half-time, the audience spilled over into the Walker lobby, where we ate exotic international foods and watched dancers with flowing veils and cymbals on their fingers. After dinner we returned for the final four hours of the play. It wasn't like any other Sunday in my life or any other theater experience.

We took both daughters to see *A Christmas Carol* when they were young, and when they were 4 and 8 years old in 1984, we sat in one of the front rows for *Guys and Dolls*. My 4-year-old spent the rest of the summer singing "I Love You, a Bushel and a Peck," and my 8-year-old announced that she wanted to become an actress. The next spring she got a small speaking role in Peter Sellars' production of *Hang on to Me*, and I learned my way around the backstage areas at the Guthrie while enduring the rigors of being a stage mother and entertaining grandparents, aunts uncles and friends who came from all over the country to share that experience with us.

During a performance of *Foxfire* in 1982, Hume Cronyn stopped the play and asked if there was a doctor in the house because a man in the audience off stage right appeared to be having some kind of health crisis. He and Jessica Tandy left the stage while doctors and paramedics ministered to the man and took him away on a stretcher. When everything had calmed down, the two actors reminded us of what had been happening in the plot before the interruption, then resumed their scene and finished the play.

I was first surprised that an actor of Cronyn's caliber, who I thought must be so absorbed in his role and blinded by stage lights, was able to see, interpret, and appropriately respond to an audience member's heart attack, but over the years I've had time to reflect on the situation. In that theater, all audience members could see and be seen. In an auditorium that wrapped most of the way around the thrust stage, nobody sat more than 45 feet from the performers. That is why the place felt so comfortable and intimate; we all felt important being there. This is why it all worked so well, and why many moments I remember from that theater on Vineland Place feel so personal.

When Tyrone Guthrie visited Minneapolis in search of a perfect place to establish a professional theater outside New York, Minneapolis, like most U.S. cities, had no professional theater. The Guthrie Theater helped put Minneapolis on the map culturally, pulling in thousands of visitors each year, thus contributing to the proliferation and success of other theaters and other arts venues throughout Minnesota. Encouraged by the Guthrie's success, dozens of other American cities established their own regional professional theaters. This influence will undoubtedly continue and grow in the coming years, as the Guthrie Theater takes its next big step.

Forty-three years after Sir Tyrone Guthrie directed the play that opened the theatre that bears his name, another production of *Hamlet* has marked that building's final important milestone.

After the last performance on May 7, 2006, the Guthrie Theater company plans to pack up and move to their new, more spacious, 3-stage facility on the banks of the Mississippi River. The theater has definitely outgrown its old building, but when the theater company moves out, the ghost of Hamlet's father will not be able to haunt the old theater on Vineland Place. The Walker Art Center, which owns the building and the land it sits on, plans to demolish it and replace it with a sculpture garden.

The city of Minneapolis has given permission to demolish the building, but preservationists have marshalled their forces to organize a protest on their web site, savetheguthrie.org. Celebrities who have performed there have added their voices to those who wish to keep and use the old building on Vineland Place, with its excellent acoustics and sight lines and its comfortable intimacy that evokes nostalgia for millions of people throughout the Midwest.

Inside the Guthrie theater on Vineland Place

The theater, designed by noted architect Ralph Rapson, is on the Minnesota Preservation Alliance's list of ten most endangered buildings and the National Trust for Historic Preservation's list of eleven most endangered buildings in the United States. Those lists raise awareness, but they don't carry any kind of legal weight.

According to an article in the *Minneapolis Tribune* on April 2, 2006, people attending *Hamlet* have been reluctant to leave after the three and a half hour performance, knowing they will not likely attend another play or concert in that space that has become so familiar, beloved, and comfortable. Ushers have had to shoo people out so they can lock up.

Despite protests from actors, musicians, architects and theater fans throughout the world who love the theater and would like to see it kept for another half century and used for concerts, conferences and plays, it will most likely be torn down. Unless an eleventh hour hero steps up to finance a reprieve, the theater will vanish from the landscape. If that happens, Minneapolis will lose one of its most beloved, comfortable, attractive and practical theatrical venues. I am sure I speak for thousands of Minnesotans when I say that we will fondly remember and greatly miss the theater on Vineland Place.

Outside the theater on Vineland Place: Courtesy of the Guthrie Theater

Irish Theater Tradition Continues in Minnesota
by Graham S. Frear

Seldom does one become so attached to a place that is not home, but no public place has become so firmly fixed in my consciousness as the Guthrie Theater. How excited and expectant were my wife Helen and I when, in 1963, we attended the inaugural performance of *Hamlet*, the uncut play with George Grizzard in the lead. With exceptions of perhaps twenty plays, we saw every play each season until my wife's death in 2001.

I continue to attend, sitting in those same seats in Aisle 3, Row 2. We always called it "the spit zone," with action and scenery often nearly in our laps and sight lines and acoustics unobstructed. Such pleasure is seldom provided in such intimate proximity to top actors and top plays in the interactive magic that is live drama.

That the theater is striking architecture we knew with pride. That one of Ireland's great producers and directors selected Minneapolis as a home for his theater seemed almost unbelievable. That the tradition continues today with another Irishman is serendipity.

Tyrone Guthrie, 1963, amidst construction of the Guthrie Theater

My great grandmother was born in Dublin, and my interest in all things Irish has been both personal and professional. I was teaching English at St. Olaf when they initiated their 4-1-4 semester configuration that offered students four classes during fall and spring semesters and one concentrated course of study in January. After a few years, the dean encouraged us to vary our routines and offer fresh courses. Irish literature had always fallen under the category of British literature, but with so many important Irish writers like O'Casey, Yeats, Beckett and Shaw, I thought it would be worthwhile to design an Irish Studies program.

My wife thought it would be smart of me to go over there and find out what I was talking about so I spent six weeks in Ireland during the summer of 1976, getting my act together and fashioning the course I would be teaching. After I taught the class for two years, I thought, "Gee, these other guys are taking their students abroad. I should take mine to Ireland." So that's what I did for the next ten years. We traveled more than 1600 miles and saw every area except Belfast.

Since it was the off-season for tourists, we were able to stay in first class hotels, and we had enough time to absorb much of the Irish culture. My wife Helen and I also spent time in Ireland.

On one of our times there, Helen and I were staying in a fine but isolated hotel converted from a palatial country home in Connemara in the west of Ireland. That night in the dining room playwright Brian Friel and his wife came in to eat. I said to Helen, "That is Brian Friel," and she asked me how I knew. "You can't miss that face," I replied. I had seen it on the book jacket of one of his plays. We were scheduled to see Friel's play, *Dancing at Lughnasa,* premier at the Abbey Theater in Dublin.

We watched as they dined and hoped they would retire to the lounge for coffee afterward, but they did not. Later that night when Helen and I came down to the bar for a nightcap, we found Mrs. Friel alone and went over and introduced ourselves. She said that Brian was on the phone and that he would join us.

When he came we introduced ourselves. He bought a round of Jameson, and we sat and talked. He told us that he had been with Tyrone Guthrie in Minneapolis for six months helping establish the form and direction of the theater in 1963. Mrs. Friel reminisced about Minneapolis and Carleton College, where Brian had been asked to speak. She said her favorite store was Dayton's.

When Joe Dowling came to Minneapolis to become artistic director of the Guthrie in 1995, we were pleased to have another Irishman at the helm. One night, looking through theater programs from performances we had seen in Dublin, I realized we had seen plays directed by Joe Dowling, including Brian Friel's *Translations*. So here we were, coming full circle.

Helen thought it would be nice to invite Joe Dowling and his wife Siobahn down to Northfield for dinner. I said, "Fat chance. They'll most likely be occupied with all the fat cats and big donors in the Twin Cities." But two weeks later I decided, well, why not? So I wrote to Joe Dowling, inviting them to dinner in our Northfield home. A week later I received a reply saying they would be happy to come, and so began a long friendship. Three decades after Brian Friel's wife expressed admiration for Dayton's, Siobahn Dowling said her favorite store in Minneapolis is Target. She said, "We have nothing like it in Ireland."

It is hard to believe that 43 years and 331 plays have graced the Guthrie Theater. It is fitting that the final play in the old theater will be *Hamlet*, bringing to full circle an achievement unequaled in American repertory theater. I recall among many memories a performance of Sophocles' *The House of Atreus*, the play about Oedipus and his tragic end. When audiences streamed out of the theater, rather than the usual ebullience and chatter, there was dead silence, the audience so touched by the shocking conclusion that they were stunned speechless. A play 2500 years old still packed its punch on a modern audience.

Helen and I returned to Ireland and spent three month-long holidays seeing plays again in Dublin and thinking how lucky we were to have a first-class theater with Irish ties in Minneapolis. Modern theater got its start at the Abbey Theater in Dublin as the brainchild of William Butler Yeats, Nobel winner in literature and his patron Lady Gregory and others. This tradition continues in Minneapolis under the sure hand of Joe Dowling and his superb repertory company.

Helen died in 2001, so to keep her memory alive in a place she so loved, I am having a seat named in her honor in the new theater, which will open in June of 2006. The new Guthrie Theater, on the banks of the Mississippi River, will be one of the great theaters in the country, if not the world. With three theaters, scene and costume shops, offices, rehearsal and dressing rooms, a full service restaurant and bar all under one handsome roof, the theater will serve its patrons well. Parking is connected by a skyway. A fourth level walkway will extend from the parking ramp through the fourth level lobby and out over the Mississippi on a breathtaking cantilevered walkway, the longest unsupported walkway in the world.

We can thank two Irishmen for our theater gem, continuing a tradition going into its forty-fourth season, where "the play's the thing." Minneapolis theater tradition continues as the ghost of Sir Tyrone hovers over Joe Dowling and his splendid new theater. As the Irish say, "Fad saol," (long life) and, "maitheas cinniuint" (good fortune.)

The new Guthrie Theater: Photo courtesy of the Guthrie Theater

Sparsely Schooled But Highly Educated
by Graham S. Frear

When one retires from teaching after years of preparing syllabi, courses, and lesson plans and facing the daily responsibility of working with hundreds of students, one retains a complex mosaic of names, faces, books and places. One remembers *Bridge on the River Kwai*, the blacksmith's cottage in *Great Expectations*, the night before Agincourt in *Henry V* and the gentle poetry of Emily Dickinson.

I taught high school for fifteen years and college English for twenty-four years. But memory of course content is of less importance than the names and faces of the many students who passed through my classroom. I was pleased when students went on to become doctors, nurses, teachers, bankers, brokers and other professionals, and certain students remain vivid in my memory.

One of my most cherished associations with a former student has been with Thomas Fliegel, academically average, but whose achievements and personality rank superlative. While his schooling may have suffered, his education was exceptional. He could accomplish practical tasks exceptionally well: make excellent scale models, construct his own house, and repair anything electronic or mechanical. Tom became a skilled mechanic, outstanding truck driver, all-around skillful carpenter and a remarkable husband and father.

After high school he worked as a mechanic and truck driver and eventually began working as a driver for Chemcentral, the largest privately owned chemical distribution company in the country. He carried hazardous chemicals, corrosives, and other components of food and industrial products, many of them dangerous to load and transport. Hundreds of products depend on these various components, from the food we eat to the medicines we use, from fuels we burn to manufactured products we depend on and use every day.

We seldom think of the cargoes of endless fleets of trucks that share our highways, crisscrossing the nation night and day, or of the drivers who keep us fed and supplied with clothing, shelter and all other supports that preserve our way of life and our futures.

Tom became one of those unsung heroes of our industrial and commercial strength who moved products by truck in hazardous weather, on glare ice, through crowded traffic, dangerous roads and speeding freeways during storms, heat and freezing temperatures. Tom told me, "I've seen it all," then continued with stories that would make the average driver blanch.

I talked to him at length about his work, his family, and of his lovely home deep in the woods of Dakota County near the small village of Hampton, where he is active in church and community. Just a month short of 35 years of driving, he retired and began drawing a good pension and medical benefits. In his backyard stands a large mobile home in which he and his wife travel to all corners of the country. He has just purchased a holiday home in Utah, a haven from Minnesota winters.

He said, "I'm very content with myself. I learned how to survive, and I had a work ethic." He completed his career with nearly three million miles of driving without accident, citation, warning or breakdown. He is one of the unsung heroes who make this country work, behind the scenes, far from the glitz of CEO high salaries and Wall Street vagaries.

Tom became the chief driver in this part of the country for his company and virtual head of its traffic department, capable of handling all aspects of the business, including the selection of new drivers and their orientation to such critical work.

He is the perfect embodiment of a highly educated technician whose schooling stopped at high school graduation but whose learning never stopped. Tom talks of his career with enthusiasm, and of his work teaching religion to youngsters in his church, and of his other community service. He and his wife look forward to summer travel, and two married children live nearby.

"I try not to call it luck," Tom says. "I earned it, and I would do it all over again." With a firm handshake and a twinkle in his eye, he always cheers my day when we meet. He has provided me with assurance that teaching school was worthwhile, that having faith in one's craft and one's students is a rewarding occupation.

Tom provided me with a valuable lesson soon after his graduation. He was a mechanic in our local Chevy garage. One bitter winter day, my car stalled several blocks from town. I walked home, called the garage, and they sent a tow truck. The driver poured a can of Heet into the tank, tried unsuccessfully to start my car, and finally towed me to the garage. Tom met us and helped push the dead car into a stall. He then stood back with his arms crossed and a big grin on his face as he said, "You know what's wrong with your car? It's out of gas. You know, Mr. Frear, there are some things they just don't teach you in school."

Thus schooling turns to wisdom, and one's student becomes teacher. These are the relationships that make teaching valuable, that enable one to share with particular students the true nature of learning and the value of wisdom that comes from experience and inner strength. Tom Fliegel was my teacher, and I merely went along for the ride.

Graham S. Frear taught English and Irish Studies at St. Olaf College, and supervised student teachers. Now retired, he enjoys a rich variety of hobbies, including art, writing poetry, and staying in touch with former students. A story about him appears on page 161. His book, "Red Shoes and Other Poems for My Wife" is available at the St. Olaf Bookstore.

Turtle Creek Adventure
by Richard Hall

Like most folks during the Great Depression, we could only afford life's bare essentials. Children learned to make do what they had and do without most things they wanted. Parents were reluctant to help kids out, and I never even heard of an allowance, so even an 8-year-old learned to be self-reliant. I always needed money, but I never had any.

One of our neighbors, feeling sorry for me, rummaged through his fishing tackle and fixed me up with a small cane pole. Of course my father wouldn't let me go fishing by myself, but if the older boys agreed to let me tag along, then I got to fish Turtle Creek.

I spent the winter of my eighth year planning for the summer ahead. I thought I was big enough to go fishing by myself, and I wanted to spend the next summer saving enough money to buy a new cane pole. I nearly pestered my father to death, trying to figure out something to do that would earn me a little money.

Finally I got the idea that selling apples might bring in some cash, but the trouble with that plan was that by the time apples ripened enough to sell, fishing season would be almost over. My father said that I could have any money that I got from selling crab apples from our tree, the only crab apple tree in our part of town. Housewives liked to make pickles and jelly from crab apples, so there was a chance I could sell a few.

Every day that summer, from the time of the blossoms, I checked those little green apples. Whenever I got the chance, I would run uptown to Decker's Hardware Store to price, admire and count their large selection of fishing poles they had leaning against the wall.

My father finally told me that the big day had arrived when I could sell crab apples. I climbed the tree and shook and shook the branches until the ground was red from all the fruit. I picked up all the best apples, put them in an orange crate in my Red Ranger wagon, and went from door to door selling a large lard pail of crab apples for ten cents.

As soon as I had enough money to buy a pole, I quit my business, ran back to my yard to park my wagon, which still had quite a few apples in it, and ran to Decker's Hardware. After studying all their poles, I found the one that I thought was the best. My boyish thinking told me that I would catch bigger fish if I had a stronger fighting line, so I bought their thickest green fish line and also a thick wire leader.

There are those who can't understand the charm of creek fishing, but for boys who never got a chance to go lake fishing, Turtle Creek was something special. It wasn't until my ninth birthday in October that my father said I could go fishing by myself, and as luck would have it, rain fell for two days.

I was a happy boy when my fishing opportunity came at last. With my new pole over my shoulder, a can of worms in my hand, and full confidence that I would catch a big fish, I started out on my first solo fishing trip, walking out to my favorite deep hole at Turtle Creek.

Two old fishermen already were fishing in my favorite spot, and although they pleasantly admired my new pole, they made it perfectly clear that they didn't want a kid fishing with them.

I moved upstream, baited my hook with a big gob of worms and threw in my line. The wind kept blowing my cork into shore, and I wasn't having any luck. I was thirsty and wanted a drink of spring water so I placed a large rock on the end of my pole and took off for Seven Springs.

On my way back, I heard the old excited fishermen calling me. I came running as fast as I could, and when I got to where I had left my pole, I saw that it was way out in the water and that it was being rapidly pulled to the other side of the creek. I jerked off my shirt and jumped into the creek, and was able to grab my pole and give it a big yank.

When I yanked the pole, the creature on the end of the line made a vigorous attempt to gain its freedom. The line sliced through the water and became so tense that I thought it would break. I kept yelling, "I've got a fish! I've got a big fish!"

A crowd of about ten people soon gathered on the bank of the creek, laughing and giving out advice and issuing threats. I remember hearing, "I'm gonna tell your father on you," and "You're going to catch your death of a cold." When I heard a neighbor woman yell, "It's that Hall kid, and he can't swim," I hoped someone might jump in and help me because I was afraid. No help arrived, however, because the water was cold and dirty.

I didn't care about the fish; I just wanted to get my new pole back. All of a sudden there was a violent jerk on the line, and my arm felt like it was pulled out. There was electricity in the air as the attention of the crowd was attracted to a rise in the water, and someone gasped, "It's no fish; it's an alligator."

Out of the swirling water came the biggest monster I had ever seen, and it was coming right at me with its jaw set. I thought I'd be eaten alive, and didn't realize that this creature hadn't seen me and probably was just as scared as I was. In self-defense, I brought my pole down hard on its back, and I heard someone yell, "It's a snapper, and its head is as big as a lard pail."

Before I knew what was happening, the turtle made a deep dive and started pulling me, kicking and screaming, towards a deep hole. I could hear people in the crowd yelling at me to let go and forget about the fishing pole, but the water was up to my armpits, and the pole was the only thing I could hold on to.

The turtle's bull-like strength had dragged me to the edge of the drop-off, and I was trembling with excitement and fatigue. I braced my feet, and with all my strength I pulled on my pole. The pole bent almost double, but I was able to bring the turtle's head to the surface, where I could see its mean eyes and open mouth.

The line stretched alarmingly tight, and the pole snapped and splintered about two feet from my hand. This gave the turtle the slack and leverage it needed. There was a big splash as I went over the drop off into the deep water. A few seconds seemed like an eternity as the turtle dragged me across the deepest part of the pond. At this point it seemed as if the turtle had caught a boy instead of a boy catching a turtle.

Finally my head popped out of the water. Coughing and choking, with water in my eyes and lungs, I found myself standing in shallow water and mud. I still had my glasses, but I had lost my pole. Someone who has never been in soft mud doesn't have an idea of the awful feeling of being sucked into the murk so I ran until I was on a sand bar.

I was sick to my stomach and distraught about my irreparable broken fishing pole. In front of all those people I had made a fool of myself, but I mustered a sense of determination and decided I was not going to quit. My parents always said I had a temper twice my size, and that's what took over as I decided to catch the turtle.

I thought the turtle had gotten away, but when I went to get my broken pole and tangled line that were still lying downstream against the creek bank, the turtle came alive again and began dragging my pole downstream. Every time I grabbed for it, he managed to keep it out of my reach. My strength was waning, and I was crazy with rage as I made one desperate grab and got hold of the pole.

Managing to stay in shallow water, I battled my way toward shore. The turtle's head kept popping out of the water, and I could see its broad back and great size as it rolled from side to side, skimmed on its side and floated and bumped along the rocks. As we reached the shallows near the shoreline, one of the old fishermen took off his shoes, rolled up his pants, and came in to help me. The tired turtle still struggled feebly as it reached a footing on the shore, and then made one last vigorous stab for freedom by kicking its flippers and striking violently,

The crowd cheered as we dragged the creature on to the shore. The turtle tried to run, but I ran after it, determined not to let it escape. Ten little fingers grabbed the shell in desperation to try to turn him over, like I had seen the fisherman do, but he was too fast and too strong. A loud, excited voice above me said, "Look out kid, you're going to get hurt," as the fisherman reached over me and flipped the turtle on its back.

Apparently this turtle had a lot of stories to tell because it had two hooks in its mouth and one in its legs. The man used my fish line to tie a stick to the turtle so it couldn't turn back over. My stomach felt like it was tied in knots, and I was quivering and blue from the cold October air.

I found my shirt and put it back on as I sat down to rest and reflect on this first solo fishing trip. The fisherman said he would guard the turtle while I went home to get my wagon. He helped me load the turtle and warned me to keep my distance from the snapper.

Some boys from the west side of town came to help me pull the wagon, and all the way home people stopped to look, and I related the whole story.

After all that I had gone through that day, the worst was still to come because I had to tell my dad what had happened. Putting it off as long as I could, I hid the wagon in a shed in the back of our house. When Dad came home for supper, he wanted to know where my pole was. I didn't know that someone had already told him the whole story as I reluctantly unfolded my adventure, trying to edit parts that I thought would upset him. When I finished my tale, I think Dad felt sorry for me because he got help, and they put the turtle in a big washtub with a board and rock on top. They guessed that the turtle weighed over 25 pounds.

I was so sad and sick to think that I had waited all summer and now I didn't have my fishing pole or anything to show for it. I would go out and poke the old turtle with a broom and say, "I'm going to eat you!" When I asked my dad when we were going to eat the turtle, he said he wasn't much for eating turtles, let alone cleaning them.

A few days later my turtle was gone. My first thought was that it had escaped, and I looked all over the neighborhood for it. When I came to supper, there was a new fishing pole where I had kept mine. Dad said that he had given the turtle away, and that the new pole was mine. My father learned from the fisherman who helped me that the turtle probably had a mate, so he played it smart and put a ten-pound test line on my pole and no leader. I spent all winter trying to figure out how I could save money to get another one of those thick green fish lines and a strong leader without having to wait for the crab apples to turn red.

This is an excerpt from "Child of the Great Depression," one of several books written and illustrated by Richard Hall, available at the Austin Historical Society. Richard and his wife Mickie live in Austin.

Fishing, Minnesota Style
by Charles A. "Tony" Burton

I'll be the first to admit that we Southerners have our own quirks as regards outdoor activities. Witness tractor pulls, demolition derbies and feral hog hunting. But when I moved to Minnesota a few years ago, I didn't know that the setting for the movie *Grumpy Old Men* really existed up there, where normally sane people go out in temperatures at or below zero, sit in little shacks on frozen waterways, and wait over a hole bored in the ice for some lethargic but desperate fish to find a dangling bit of bait attractive.

When my wife and I were driving around, she would point out to me the barely chilled lakes in November, and tell me how, when they froze to a sufficient depth, their surfaces would be dotted with the shrines of the faithful, i.e., the ice fishermen.

This was my first experience with a Minnesota winter. I had to buy and install an engine-block heater to keep my oil liquid on cold nights, so my Jeep would start in the morning. I went out and bought a pair of "bad weather boots" and an Arctic-style parka so I could go out in this frigid purgatory. Even with those, however, I never stayed out for very long. My Southern blood just didn't seem to take it very well, I guess.

I didn't like it when, walking to the video rental store one night, my eyes were watering badly from the cold and the frames of my glasses literally froze to my cheeks and nose from the tears. My beard and mustache were glazed over with ice from my breath, and crackled when I spoke. Usually I was saying, "Aaarrghhh… c-c-c-cooooollldd," or some similar intelligent observation.

But up here, this is the winter norm, so I should not have expected to be too surprised at ice fishing. As I went to the malls and to Wal-Mart, I began to see signs of the ice fishing phenomenon. For instance, they were selling ice augers, huge hand-operated drill bits that are made to open a fishing hole through the ice that is twelve inches and thicker.

And there were these little flimsy contrivances like tents, which I was told were portable ice-fishing houses. They looked like a good wind, similar to the ones I was beginning to experience on my walks outside, would take them over any convenient rainbow faster than Dorothy ever thought of going.

As the lakes and rivers began to freeze thicker, I started noticing small sheds appearing on their frozen surfaces. They looked exactly like outhouses, with the only differences being that they did not have a crescent moon cut into the door, and they had little chimneys that spouted thin plumes of smoke. After two or three fishermen spend all day in there with a bucket of bait staying thawed over a can of Sterno, they probably smell worse than most outhouses. The ice-fishing shacks, I mean, not the fishermen.

Lake Superior, however, which contains fully 10% of all the earth's fresh water and was visible from the back door of my apartment, remained only partially frozen until early in January. About the middle of January, we drove over into Wisconsin, a journey of only a few miles. A very brisk wind was blowing out of the north, across Lake Superior.

Lara, my wife, said to me, "Look, see the ice fishermen?" I looked, and could hardly believe it. There were about twelve to fifteen ice fishing houses out on the lake. Beside them were heavily bundled humans – I assume they were human because they had vaguely human form. There were also several vehicles out on the ice. Now, this was not close to the shore. These pickups, minivans, 4x4s and small passenger cars were hundreds of yards out on the lake. Some were even driving around, at speeds that looked to be around 35 miles per hour.

I know from experience how hard it is to stop if the road is just coated with a thin glaze of ice. What must it be like to stop on pure ice, with no chains or studded tires? And what if you hit a thin spot, where there was some hidden current wearing away at the ice? I didn't even want to try it.

But I did want to get some pictures, so I got the digital camera and stepped out of the car onto the shore of Lake Superior. Although it was sunny, the ambient temperature that day was about 4 degrees Fahrenheit. The wind off the lake was whipping along at a speed of around 25-35 miles per hour, giving us a wind chill factor of minus 18 to 22 degrees.

I gasped when it hit me, the wind scraping my throat like sandpaper. Resolute soul (or idiot) that I was, I went right down to the water's... um, ice's edge, and proceeded to take some pictures. There they were, the dedicated and faithful, seeking out the wily smelt, pike and walleye. They were also seeking out the warmest spot in their little sheds, and seeking to consume a fair quantity of alcohol.

Although it is a sport with little activity (basically, you sit for hours on a camp stool over a hole in the ice and wait for some hungry fish to take your bait), it is dangerous. There were at least 20 deaths related to ice fishing in Minnesota and Wisconsin the last year I lived there, most from carbon monoxide poisoning or exposure. And you have to watch the ice. Sometimes, it can get rotten overnight, and the intrepid sportsman may find that his little home-away-from-home has sunk into the lake or river where he intended to fish. There were often stories in the local papers about this happening, two or three times each season.

I got back into my car and managed to unwrap my stiffened fingers from around the camera. I cleaned the ice glaze from my glasses, and soaked up the heat coming from the vents in my Jeep. I closed my eyes and remembered with longing, pulling catfish and small mouth bass from the warm waters of a Georgia lake, and with a sigh I headed home to my apartment.

I am back in Georgia now, and I often walk to a recreational lake about a mile from my home. There, I paddle a johnboat out onto the lake, and spend a leisurely afternoon pulling bream, crappie and the occasional catfish or small mouth bass from the water. But, I do miss the more distinct change of seasons in Minnesota, and those frosty mornings when the only sensible thing to do seems to be to stay in bed and snuggle. So, we return for the occasional visit to my wife's parents and siblings, revel in the deep snow for a few days, and make admiring noises about the snowmen and snow forts our nieces and nephews build in the yard. Ultimately, though, I am a Southerner, and as beautiful as Minnesota in wintertime may be, the pull of the magnolia and honeysuckle is just too strong for me to resist.

"Tony Burton grew up in Georgia, but moved to Minnesota after meeting his wife who lived in Duluth. He and Lara now live in Georgia, where he is an author and publisher.

My Skates and Mrs. Dunleavy--Whoops!
by Marion L. Forderbrugen

I loved roller-skating around the block or just up and down in front of our house on Front Street in Mankato. It was something I could do alone if the other kids weren't around to play with. My skates were the clamp-on kind, with a skate key that I wore on a string around my neck. I had to carry it with me because if the skates came loose from my shoes, I had to tighten them up with the key.

When I got through skating each day, Mom always told me to put my skates in the front closet so no one would fall on them. One day I came in and Mom wasn't home to remind me, and my memory wasn't working. I took my skates off just inside the dining room by the kitchen door, and there I left them.

Later I was upstairs, and I heard someone calling quietly. I ran down because I had thought I was alone in the house. In the dining room lay Mrs. Dunleavy with her head under Mom's buffet. The bottom of the buffet was higher in the center and tapered to the sides. I rang the little bell to the print shop in our basement and yelled for Dad to come.

Our Mankato house on Front Street

Was I in big trouble! Mrs. Dunleavy had come downstairs from where she had been napping, and she tripped on my skates and fell with her head going under the center of the buffet. When she turned over to try to get up, her head was trapped under the narrow end.

It was awful! I thought I had killed her, but she was talking. Dad moved her back to the center and gently pulled her out and got her on her feet. All the while I watched this rescue, I was shaking in my shoes because I knew it was my fault for leaving my skates out. She was a tiny lady, not much taller than I was, and I felt terrible.

When Mom got home and found out what had happened, she said she was taking my skates away. I had it coming, but Mrs. Dunleavy heard Mom and came to my rescue. She said it was just an accident, and I didn't mean to make her fall. With a stern warning I got my skates back, and after that I always put them in the closet after skating.

Each time I look at a picture of that tiny lady in my old photo album, I remember that awful day when I could have killed her and lost my skates--all in the same day.

Rochester resident Marion Forderbrugen has written journals, a poetry book, and books for her family about growing up in Mankato. She enjoys the company of her poodle, Tinkerbell.

The Story Behind Bob's Triangle
by John Peters

The farm David Peters and his family lived on was about five miles south of St. Cloud. There were seven children, and I was one of them, but the two we are interested in finding out more about for this story are Bob, who was about 8 years old and Stanley, who was around 13. In those prehistoric times, children discovered their own means of fun, excitement, and entertainment.

Stanley had a gun that had a practical use for target practice and hunting. But if these activities got dull after awhile, he had to figure out something more exciting.

What Stan had in mind when he started out that day is anybody's guess. He had a .22 gauge rifle, and the two kinds of shells available for that gun were the solid bullet and the multiple, so-called bird shot that contained many tiny pellets. Stan had some of these, and while experimenting he discovered that if he took out the pellets, he would have a shell that went "bang," without firing any projectile material.

What did he have in mind that day when he headed out with one of those empty-headed shells? I am not sure, but I think it was some kind of power play. While Stan and his little brother stood in the shed between the kitchen and the outside, Stan pointed the gun at Bob's butt and commanded Bob to dance. Bob did not move. Again Stan gave the command, but in a more assertive tone of voice. Again Bob failed to respond.

"Bang!" went the gun. Bob jumped three feet in the air and headed screaming for the house. Stanley jumped six feet and headed for the barn. A little detective work revealed three pellets embedded in Bob's butt, arranged in a triangle pattern. These became permanent fixtures for the rest of his life.

Apparently when Stan removed the pellets, he missed three. I don't remember what the punishment was because I was only about 4 years old, but I heard the story many times and grew up believing the old saying that guns by themselves are not harmful. It's when people and guns get together that they become dangerous.

A Family Experience
by John Peters

By the time my wife Nadine and I had been married ten years, we had three children, and we were enjoying our lives as farmers. After renting various farms over the years, and moving five times in six years, we had an opportunity to buy a farm in the southern part of Sterns County between Eden Valley and Paynesville, and we took the plunge.

Dairy farming provided our main income. This involved the regular job of milking twice a day, and in order to keep from going dry, the cows had to have a calf every year. Usually calving happened without a problem, but occasionally a cow needed a little help accomplishing this miracle.

This particular morning, Tillie was in the calving mood. Tillie was a heifer, which means this was her first calf. We decided to put her in a pen by herself, where she would be able to move about freely while we kept a close eye on her while we went about our customary milking chores. We had to stay on course to finish by the time the truck arrived to pick up the milk.

By breakfast time it appeared that Tillie was making no progress, and I made a mental note to check up on her in a short time. When you work an hour or more before breakfast, your appetite becomes really sharp, and Nadine had breakfast ready as our girls came downstairs to eat with us. We had no problems with finicky girls not eating at our place. Their lives were so active that their appetites were naturally strong.

The five of us started conversing, and the kids wanted to know what was going on in the barn. When I told them about Tillie, Nadine said, "This is a family affair, so let's go see."

When we got to the barn to check Tillie, nothing had happened. Since I had no experience in cow midwifing, we decided to play it by ear. In those difficult Depression years you didn't call a vet at the first sign of difficulty. You exhausted your wisdom and common sense first.

"I believe you should check the birth canal," Nadine suggested.

"Will do," I replied, and when we proceeded to do that, we discovered the calf's feet just out of sight, and when we proceeded further, we discovered the calf's head was turned backwards. As we shared our findings with the girls, we tried to put them at ease. Nadine and I decided the best thing to try was to force the calf back far enough to loosen the problem, and we hoped this would allow Tillie to birth her baby naturally.

Yep, in about five minutes, Tillie's baby was on the pen floor and trying to stand up. The yells of joy from the girls were ecstatic. "Come on, Mama," I said. "Let's you and me go have a cup of coffee together. These girls will share what happened in their own language."

Oldest to youngest: Judy, Joanne, Sara Jane, Phyllis, Debbie Peters on their farm in Sterns County.

Owatonna resident John Peters, age 91, retired from farming and became a meat cutter in grocery stores at Paynesville, Owatonna and Blooming Prairie. He and his wife Nadine raised five daughters, who now live in five different states.

Fowl Play
by Jeri L. Blazek

My husband Mike and his brother were in Owatonna's Morehouse Park sometime in their teens, either enjoying the day or up to no good. I never asked. Whatever the case, he was near the dam where people enjoy throwing in their fishing lines to see what the Straight River might produce, and a kid who looked like he was about 6 years old appeared, wearing just a pair of shorts, no shirt or shoes, and covered with reddish welts. The two older guys were very concerned and asked the kid what happened.

The boy smiled, and I always imagine him without a tooth or two, although Mike has never rendered that detail. "I caught a goose," he said. As the story unfolds, Mike explains that the kid had sat behind some foliage or a garbage can or something until a goose waddled by. Then he jumped out, grabbed the bird, and "just held on."

In my family, this story is legendary. And every time Mike retells it, usually at my insistence as I laugh and clap, everyone enjoys and understands it. But this is only one family story about the waterfowl and their relation to people in that park.

Morehouse Park sits slightly to the west of the center of Owatonna. The Straight River and the Kaplan's Woods Parkway Trail border the park, which houses playground equipment, a pavilion, baseball diamond, drinking fountains, a chalet and several man-made duck ponds. In the winter, the river is groomed for ice-skating, winter bonfires, and years ago, for broom ball games. The small duck ponds serve as overflow sheets of ice. For most of the year, Morehouse Park also serves host to a thriving duck and goose population.

If there is one thing my family will do when faced with a large number of animals standing around, it's throw food at them. Feeding the ducks was a wholesome, cheap family activity that we participated in regularly. It wasn't like we were on a schedule or anything, but every so often we'd grab some old bread, popcorn, or expired Cheerios and head for the park. We fed ducks on special days too, such as Mother's Day or when my grandfather visited from Kansas.

There are several styles of duck feeding, and each one is really just a matter of preference. I usually spread the feed wide and then try to make sure that the ducks on the fringe of the frenzy get some as well. These outer ducks are shy and sometimes scrawny. I almost have to chase after them to make sure they get some of the bounty.

My mother fed ducks out of her hand. She would crouch down and be still with food in hand until some of the bold or hungry ducks would sidle up, squaring off to see if the threat of this human was worth the treasure. Most often any duck that ate out of my mother's hand soon sensed there was no danger and gorged itself to her delight. As any duck feeder will attest, one important thing to do is to throw enough food far enough out so that the geese, with their mean, spit-hissing beaks, remain satisfied and don't move into the immediate audience. I've seen more than one amateur backed up on a picnic table surrounded by geese until she throws down her bag of bread crumbs and escapes while the geese are diverted.

Young Jeri Blazek with her mom and brother, LaGene and Mikel Akers.

The Owatonna Public Utilities, particularly the meter shop where I work, butts up to Morehouse Park. We often use the park's pavilion for union meetings or retirement parties. One summer a coworker and I rescued three goslings that had found their way into a storm sewer of the cooling tower.

Goslings are much easier to deal with, and much better-natured than their adult counterparts. These guys were fuzzy, creamy yellow, and their cheeping voices touched our hearts. We kept them in a five-gallon bucket over our lunch break, and my crew fed them bread crusts and other bits of lunch.

After lunch, my partner and I drove my utility vehicle into the park and released the goslings into a duck pond that was teeming with brand new duck families. The duck mom that we zeroed in on spooked and headed to the center of the pond as we approached, but after we released the babies and backed away, she turned back to shore and let our orphans jump into the line with her own brood of four or five in tow. My coworker looked at me and said, "She's a good mom."

Yeah, she sure was.

Jeri Blazek lives in rural Claremont with her husband and two dogs. She has taught English and creative writing for Minnesota State University and Riverland Community College.

River Rise
by Michael Finley

Seven forty-five a.m. today, along the Mississippi in Saint Paul, a mile south of Fort Snelling:

It was a remarkable thing to see. My dog Beau is trotting down a path he has walked a hundred times. The woods there are paved with brown cottonwood leaves, papered together by autumn rains. They are nearly one thing now, a loose carpet of leaves. Then, suddenly, the carpet gives way under Beauregard, and he sinks into the river below. The river, as it rose, lifted the entire forest carpet in one piece. The dog's weight has punched a hole in the illusion. It is like disappearing into a mirror.

I am fascinated by rising water. Looked at from a distance, the river is a single sheet of water. But it has an edge that is usually very small--a rivulet of water moving forward a tablespoon at a time. If you can find this exploring tongue of water, you can walk alongside it as it leads the river to new places, like a bull on a ring.

You understand geology better. These hills you tramped over so many times are no longer hills once the water rises. They are sandy islands, fashioned from the slabs of sand deposited from an earlier flood, then rolled round and hilly by the currents of this one.

Floods are a killing evil to human communities, but the river never asked us to establish ourselves on its banks. Upriver, the water sweeps things away one layer at a time, like a grocer cleaning his shelves. One time, I looked out by the hydroelectric station under the Ford Parkway Bridge to see a flotilla of white plastic bleach jugs bobbing their way downstream--thousands of them, gawking like stiff-necked tourists.

As a puppy, Beauregard benefited from floods. The November day we brought him home it snowed, and that winter was the snowiest in Minnesota ever. All winter he stayed indoors and learned civilized ways. Then, when the snows melted, and the river rose, they sealed the flooded parklands off from traffic, and the riverbanks were ours to wander.

In the spring of 1997, the crest of the river passing through Minneapolis was topped with plastic shopping bags. Since they were the high point at the moment water levels fell, the bags impaled themselves at the 18 feet above flood stage level. Plastic bags filled trees and bushes, but only at a certain height, like a ghostly garland hung along the wooded shore, or bleached laundry clothespinned on a line. It took the breezes of several summers for those bags to tear free and undo their effect.

There is a pond by the Crosby Farm, one of the first settlements in the state, where park workers had built a walkout of stout beams and steel pontoons. Many times we would walk past that massive raft, where Hmong men and their sons caught sunnies and crappies for supper.

In the flood of 1997, the river completely swamped that pond, and the raft vanished. A year later, Beau and I were cutting through some brush a mile and a half from the pond, and we found the pontoon raft, perched against an immense cottonwood trunk, its steel barrels staved in, and the giant beams splintered asunder. The flood had transported it in the night and set it against the tree.

It's all filthy. When the river tips, it abolishes separation. River water, drinking water, sewer water, rain water, waste water, gasoline from cars and underground reservoirs, and the fluids sucked from sodden cemeteries all flow together and form a common army. Once the flood lies down on your mattresses, you don't want your mattresses back.

What is most astonishing to me is how the river comes roaring back each time. A year after Pike Island was almost entirely submerged under a tide of this filth, it was a paradise of green. All the deadwood was swept away, and all that remained was shot full of light.

The only downside was that, in the aftermath of uprooting, certain weeds like stinging nettles gained a foothold, and now they dominate the forest floor, making it impossible to walk through in short pants or bare arms in the summertime.

In the wake of the flood, the animals become bolder. Beavers establish themselves within earshot of the city. I have seen coyotes prowling the scrub near the coal-burning plant. Snapping turtles venture inland to lay their eggs in dry soil. Blue herons soar just below the airport. The deer stare boldly at you, because you cannot get to them.

Think of the carp that swam into a new inlet made by the rushing water; how happy they were to eat bugs and plants which had never before been underwater. And now unhappy they will be a few days hence, when the flood recedes, and their way out is sealed up, and the sun goes to work, and the oxygen in the puddle is depleted, and the liquid seeps into the sand.

The river is rearranging the furniture of the world. Wait, until the new order becomes clear.

St. Paul resident Michael Finley has worked as a newspaperman in Worthington, a TV producer for the University of Minnesota, and a columnist for the St. Paul Pioneer Press. For more of his writing, visit his website http://mfinley.com.

Soderbeck's Ferry
by Dorman Lehman

Today a little used gravel road leads east from Pine City, past small farms, to end at the bank of the St. Croix River. Not too many years ago this road didn't end at the river, but continued on to Grantsberg, Wisconsin, with a steady flow of traffic, for here was Soderbeck's Ferry.

The ferry was a small, low, two-car barge, looking a bit like a wooden bridge with low iron side rails. The landing ramps bent and groaned when used by even the small cars of the day. Some of the deck boards were loose and she leaked, but Soderbeck's Ferry was to me the grandest vessel between Minnesota and Wisconsin.

Soderbeck's was more than just the ferry. There was a big farmhouse beside the road, with its well-tended garden, and an icehouse, where cold blocks of pure river ice lay beneath great dunes of warm sawdust. The area was dotted with tents of Twin City friends and cabins of weekend or summer visitors, and there was the old sawmill.

The sawmill consisted of an endless expanse of wooden sheds, concrete foundations, roller conveyors, gears and cables and machinery that a boy could explore for days. Almost hidden in a corner of the main shed was the community pump, which when properly primed, yielded water just one degree above freezing. You were expected to refill the priming coffee can for the next camper.

And there was Soderbeck himself. I never heard anyone use his first name, or any sort of title, but to me he was king of all this, and I liked him. He must have liked kids, for he had the most complete set (eight boys and six girls) I have ever known. He was a little man at least a hundred years old, and walked with a limp, caused, as far as I could tell, from wearing boots with one sole built up 3 or 4 inches. I never mentioned this to him.

Soderbeck tolerated my endless questions about the sawmill, the ferry and the river. He ignored my advice about gardening, but marveled at my few small fish. He was also properly impressed with my new, Fourth of July six guns, and he let me ride on the ferry.

He taught me how to adjust the chains to the upstream cable so the current would help propel the ferry. He showed me how to "walk" the lower cable the length of the hull, and let go soon enough so as not to be left dangling above open water. Whenever the hull needed pumping out, he even let me operate the giant upright pump handle, back and forth, until from somewhere deep below would come the slurping sounds of the last few drops.

Those frequent weekend days at Soderbeck's were paradise with swimming, exploring, berry picking, hunting arrowheads, fishing just around the bend below the sawmill or being allowed to go fishing up river with the big people. The sights were grand and the smells were even better: the canvas of our tent, wood and grease of the sawmill, pine trees, fish from the river, wood smoke and coffee.

But the evenings were the best of all. Late on a warm summer night, after we had heard the eight o'clock whippoorwill, the last cup of coffee had been drained into the campfire, the fish all cleaned and the day's events had been exaggerated to the limit, I would lie in our tent and listen to the night.

Soderbeck's landing near Pine City

From somewhere across the river an auto horn would sound, and I would lift the tent flap to see headlights flickering through the trees. A screen door would slam.

I would hear Soderbeck's footfalls and then the sound of the ferry scraping away from the landing. It would silently drift across the dark river, and then after another memorized sequence of sounds, float back to shore. Headlights would dust away in the darkness, a screen door would slam, and all would be quiet again. As I fell asleep, I would wonder about that late night traveler-- a hired hand bringing the farmer's daughter home before midnight, one of the gangsters of that day, or perhaps a father with a boy like me seeking some place to camp for the night.

The convenience of new bridges and paved roads put an end to the need for Soderbeck's Ferry. The Second World War put an end to my visits there, and time has deprived us of Soderbeck. But whenever I hear a whippoorwill or a lonesome auto horn in the night, I remember.

Dorman Lehman grew up in the Twin Cities and Grand Rapids areas. After some years in the housing industry, he began directing history museums. Now retired, he does historical research and some consulting.

Aunt Ruthie and the Minnesota Twins
by Carolyn Smith

Growing up in Britt, Iowa, my two sisters and I eagerly anticipated any occasion that might warrant a visit from our city-dwelling Aunt Ruthie. She was everything we wanted to be.

The three of us blond, blue-eyed little girls were often photographed in a stair step fashion, me the tallest and oldest by four years, Ginny, in the middle, and two years later, Janet. I have often considered having no brothers a handicap in terms of figuring out the opposite sex. Poor Dad was outnumbered and had no one to play catch with or teach how to fish. Instead he was invited to attend tea parties and judge beauty pageants, and his house was littered with paper dolls.

Our father, Warren Paige, was a Methodist minister. He grew up in Waterloo, Iowa. When he was a baby, his father was electrocuted throwing a switch on the railroad. His mother died when he was in seminary.

My mother, Irene Arrasmith, from Cherokee, Iowa, was also the oldest of three girls, but their upbringings were quite different. There were Irene, Ruthie and Helen. Mom's last memory of her mother, my grandmother, was a small wave from the passenger side window of the car as she left for the hospital to give birth to Helen. When she died, my grandfather, in what must have been a state of overwhelming grief and confusion, gave Helen away for adoption. Fortunately, Helen's adoptive parents believed she should have contact with her father and sisters, so there were occasional visits and correspondence by mail. Aunt Florence came by train from Kentucky with her favorite cut-glass bowl on her lap to raise my mother and Ruthie, efficiently, if not affectionately. My only remaining grandparent died when I was just an infant.

My parents met in college in Iowa City. After graduating, they married and moved to Evanston, Illinois, where my father attended seminary. My orphaned parents relied almost solely on each other. When Dad reminisced about their courtship, he would croon, "Good Night, Irene" in his mellow tenor voice. They held hands while watching black and white TV and accepted that life was as it should be—male and female, created equal but with very different roles.

His role was to win souls for Christ. Hers was to support him in his ministry. Mom washed and pressed Dad's white shirts into crisp, bright reflections of his respected position in the community. She would deliver the program at the Women's Society of Christian Service, and then run home to "punch down" the bread dough. She sewed for us, but she made do with the same dress by adding or removing bows and belts.

My mother had one leg shorter than the other, so she had to have the heel of one shoe built up, and she always struggled to keep up with my fast-walking father.

Mom's sister Ruthie's burden in life was diabetes. My mother remembers when Ruthie was quite young that the needle broke off when someone was giving her insulin, which necessitated a trip to the doctor. I imagine that Ruthie's illness put her in the forefront in terms of the family's attention and relegated Mom to the background, a place she was to occupy for her whole life. Ruthie married Chuck Stewart, and they lived in Montana, where they both worked for the American Lung Association. Just before he died of lung cancer, he saw Jesus standing at the foot of his bed.

Alone and childless, with health problems of her own, Ruthie started over in Minneapolis, working in a bank for a few years. When a friend knew a friend who was leaving a job as executive secretary for Calvin Griffith, then owner of the Minnesota Twins, Ruthie applied. Calvin was impressed with her knowledge of the Twins—she was a fan. She began a whirlwind career behind the scenes, which included an annual working vacation at spring training in Orlando.

Ruthie was a superb example of a sophisticated working woman, a regular Mary Tyler Moore. She always had a great tan, perfect make-up and hair-do, wore expensive clothes and dated lots of men. When she visited us in our home, she polished our fingernails and styled our hair, teasing and spraying until our coifs were protected from the sharpest of Iowa winds, all the time talking to my mother about someone fabulous she had just met. When we went to church, we always felt that everyone was looking at us, wondering who that beautiful woman was, sitting with the preacher's family. She must be rich, we knew they were thinking, and she was ours, all ours, at least for the weekend.

Back at home we followed Aunt Ruthie around like puppies and pestered her with questions. She always said yes when we asked if we could watch while she gave herself an insulin injection. Just the thought of going to the doctor to get a shot was enough to make me hide in a closet, so I was amazed that she could do it herself.

My sisters and I thought Ruthie's gifts were spectacular. One Christmas we got bright colored animal print flannel pajamas with feet. When we modeled them for a photo, we looked like a promotional poster for the musical *Cats*. Another time she gave us beautiful music boxes. Mine was shiny black and painted with oriental designs. When I opened it, a tiny ballerina with a pink tutu popped up and twirled around in time to the music. I wish I still had it or could remember what song it played. I do still have the sleek black gloves with mink trim that Ruthie gave me when I was in high school. She was the only person I knew who actually owned a fur coat.

When Mom and Dad took us to visit Ruthie in the Twin Cities, our eyes were opened wide. The miles of crisscrossing roads, cars rushing everywhere, and skyscrapers taller than we had ever seen before were frightfully exciting.

I was mostly impressed with the sirens—police, ambulance, fire trucks. In the small Iowa towns of my growing up, sirens were big news, and people came out of their houses and stores to see where the emergency crews were headed. In the Cities, it seemed there was always a crisis, and every time another siren wailed, my heart quickened and I wondered who it was, what was wrong, and whether or not someone was dying, right at that very minute.

Ruthie gave us a tour of the business offices of the Minnesota Twins at Metropolitan Stadium in Bloomington and proudly introduced us to her boss, a large-faced, many-chinned, round man, who had a huge, blue fish on the wall behind his desk. Years later in the same office my father-in-law said to Mr. Griffith, "You buy and sell players the way we buy and sell hogs."

He answered, "We try not to think of it that way."

Before the game, Ruthie always treated us to lunch in the company cafeteria. I felt any minute a celebrity might walk in, but even when she introduced us to someone, I didn't really know who he was. Sports were just not a big part of our growing up, and it had never occurred to me to read about baseball in the newspaper or pay attention when adults were talking. My only clue that we were in the presence of greatness was by listening to what Ruthie said, and I accepted it all as gospel.

Metropolitan Stadium was bigger than the biggest church I'd ever been in, a jumble of moving colors and sounds. We watched the Twins from the players' wives' section, and even if I got bored watching the game, I never tired of watching people. I was impressed at the wives' nonchalance—they mostly sat and read books and only paid attention when their husbands were up to bat. Ruthie told us what she thought of each player. Al Worthington, Harmon Killebrew, Rod Carew, she knew them all. Harmon, she said, was a peach of a guy.

In August of 1965, the summer before my senior year, my friend Kathy and I took the Greyhound bus from Mason City to Minneapolis to visit Aunt Ruthie. It was the first time I had ever traveled without my parents. Ruthie had to work while we were there, but we enjoyed our leisure time. Apartment living was chic to us, and Ruthie hung her pictures at eye level, the latest in home decor. We loved sitting by the swimming pool, hoping to see cute boys, and playing cards. I learned how to shuffle so the cards made a fluttering sound as they slid back into place.

After work Ruthie took us shopping or to a game. We saw the Twins, again from the players' wives' section. We saw the Vikings play Philadelphia from a private box, where waitresses brought anything we wanted to eat or drink. Best of all, we saw that new rock 'n roll sensation from England, the Beatles, in concert. We were really smug when we entered the stadium through the office doors, mobbed by fans who thought that might be where the Beatles were hiding. I can still hear our screams and the funny way Paul McCartney pronounced "Minneapolis."

Ruthie was a big part of my life even after I grew up, married, and became a Minnesotan just like her. My husband Greg loves baseball. I often thought he married me just because he liked talking baseball with Ruthie. We went to many Twins games, once sharing a box with Senator

Hubert H. Humphrey. The line-up for autographs in the aisle made it hard to see the game, but it was his son Skip's wedding day, so he had to leave the game early.

Ruthie doted on our daughter, Holly. When Holly was two and we were visiting, she almost choked on a penny. Until Greg shook her upside down and the penny fell out, I thought the next siren would be for us.

I loved and admired Ruthie, but I always felt that, had a fairy godmother arrived on the scene, Ruthie would have changed places with my mother in an instant, even though from my vantage point my mother's life was boring. Mom never wore make-up other than lipstick, but she had what Ruthie wanted—a husband and family of her own.

The most independent thing my mother ever did was to fly to Florida all by herself to be with Ruthie when she became ill. Ruthie had left the Minnesota Twins to take a new job because if you weren't a Griffith, you really didn't have any chance to advance in the organization. One day she didn't show up for work. Someone in her apartment complex found her lying naked on the floor, half under her bed. The mirror above her dresser was broken, and on the floor next to her was a hammer and unopened bottles of medicine—the kind with childproof caps, still securely fastened.

Mom and Helen stayed with Ruthie until Dad just missed Mom too much and she had to come home. It was congestive heart failure and other complications of diabetes, and somehow it was decided that she could no longer live alone. She moved to the Chicago area to live with Helen and her three daughters. Several years later, Helen found Ruthie dead in her bed at age 54. I had just sent her a get-well card because I heard she hadn't been feeling well. It arrived the following day, too late.

Ruthie and my sister Janet were my son Kyle's baptism sponsors. I cherish the photos of that day. Helen and her family were there too, and of course Dad did the baptizing. Kyle never had the privilege of knowing Ruthie, but like his dad and grandpa, he loves baseball. When Kyle was in sixth grade, Greg took him out of school early to see the Twins defeat the Cardinals, 10 to 1, in the first game of the 1987 World Series.

As I watched the game on TV, I imagined that Ruthie was there, at the Hubert H. Humphrey Metrodome, enjoying the noise and waving her Homer Hanky. She would have loved it that Harmon threw out the first pitch. She would have told Kyle insider stories about Frank Viola, Kirby Puckett, and Dan Gladden, who hit a grand slam home run that night.

A few days later, after the sixth game of the Series, Greg and I were walking away from the Metrodome, our voices gone and nearly deaf from Kent Hrbek's grand slam in the sixth inning. There across the street, about to get into a sparkling white Lincoln, was an older Calvin Griffith. He was no longer the owner of the Twins, but people were lined up to talk to him. We got in line, and when it was our turn I told him I was Ruthie Stewart's niece, not knowing for sure if he'd even remember her. "She used to bring my sisters and me to your office," I said.

He thought a moment. "Oh, yes, I remember," he said, "three little blond girls."

Ruthie's life seemed incredibly exciting to a small town girl from Iowa, but now, when I think of her, I just feel sad. I remember she said she had once come "that close" to meeting ol' blue eyes himself, Frank Sinatra, at a party. Her life was like that. Ruthie's dreams may not have been realized, but she was more than "that close" for us.

Ruthie Stewart

Carolyn Smith lives on a farm near Alden. She and Greg have two adult children.

Best Christmas Ever
by Florence H. Kohn

When I was 12 years old and my sister was 6, we had the best Christmas I ever remember. We were not allowed to open our gifts on Christmas Eve, as some families did. We had to wait until after church on Christmas so by the time we got home from church we were pretty excited about opening them.

Our excitement paid off because we got a wonderful surprise that Christmas. In those days we had a lot of snow in Wabasha, and we kids got a toboggan for Christmas. All the other kids we knew had sleds, but ours was the only toboggan. In the afternoon, after our Christmas dinner, we all went over to Barton's Hill to slide on the road. There weren't many cars on that road in those days so playing there was safer than it sounds like it would be.

Times were hard in the '30s, but my dad must have hit the jackpot that year because he gave Mom a beautiful floor lamp with prisms on the shade. She also received a fox fur neck scarf, which was very stylish in those days. I guess Dad must have shot the fox and had the hide and fur made into a scarf for her. Boy, we sure were lucky and happy.

It's been a long time since my twelfth Christmas, but there are still folks in town who remember my toboggan. It's amazing how much I remember about that Christmas, the most memorable one of my life. What made it so special was that we didn't only get things we needed, but we also got things we wanted.

Florence Kohn still lives in Wabasha. She enjoys writing stories and submitted her work because of the encouragement of the Wabasha Public Library staff.

Armistice Day Blizzard
by Florence H. Kohn

November 11, 1940, started out as a warm, calm day. My husband and I had plans to put storm windows on our apartment. I got busy and washed them so they would be ready to put up when he got home from work, but the weather changed in a hurry.

By the time he got home, it was windy, snowing and cold. I don't remember how much the mercury fell, but it fell fast. We could hardly hold the windows to put them on the house, but we got the job done as the blizzard moved into Wabasha.

With our work all done, my husband and I, who had been married about a year, decided to go out and have fun so we walked two blocks to a dance at our Legion Hall. We knew it was cold and windy, and it was rough going as we walked home from the dance, but we went anyway.

We didn't know it at the time, but while we were having a good time, country folks with livestock to take care of and people traveling on country roads were bearing the brunt of the storm, and many were stranded. We had a radio, but communication wasn't like it is now with reporters going out in a storm to keep listeners up to date. We knew it was snowing and we knew it was bad, but some of us in town didn't really understand the extent of the storm until the next day.

The next day we learned about the death and destruction caused by that storm. Since it was Armistice Day and a Monday, some businesses had been closed and many sportsmen were enjoying a long weekend. Many duck hunters were out on the Mississippi and in the low lands near Wabasha, and several were stranded and some even died.

Across the state 27 people died, including 11 duck hunters. I think one man lost his life on the trestle bridge at Read's Landing. How foolish it was for us to go out dancing while all those people were suffering in the storm, but we were young, and that was our fun and entertainment in those days.

A Tough Sale
by Ted Springer

As an introvert, selling magazines door to door struck me as a bad idea, akin to the Saturday night bath. No, even worse. Dad and Mom said I'd learn to be a good businessman and earn lots of money. That appealed to them, dear souls, coming off the difficult Depression years. It didn't appeal a whole lot to me. Being a shortstop did appeal to me--or maybe even becoming a running back for the Minnesota Gophers someday. I was 11 years old, and the thought of...gulp...selling something was, well, sort of life-threatening.

But these were trying years. The family was eating lots of Spam and hoping Dad wouldn't get laid off. I was used to putting cardboard in my shoes to cover the holes--wasn't everyone?

Mom had taken a sales job at Powers Department Store in downtown Minneapolis to help out, and I knew it was tough for her. Not only did she have bad feet, aggravated by hours of standing, but also having graduated from a "la dee dah" Eastern women's school, Smith College, she had hopes of making her positive mark in life in a far more global way.

I well remember the first time the magazines were dropped off, ready for sale, at our duplex. The year was 1940, and the magazine was *Liberty*. The circulation man who brought them was a brusque, jowly, built like a brick you-know-what kind of guy. He was nice enough, but in my mind he was thinking, "You'd better produce, kid, because the world is watching, and if you fail, you'll never play shortstop."

I set out to sell, not knowing just where or how to start because nobody had taught me the first step toward becoming a mogul. Not wanting to take advantage of friends, I ventured into adjacent neighborhoods--like Joan Hilpert's. Joan, a friend from Sidney Pratt grade school, always tried to kiss me (ugh!). She had a white chow dog that liked to eat ankles of kids who rode by on their bikes. I learned early on that when I rode past her house, I had to generate lots of speed, pull my legs up, and coast beyond chow range--and kissing range too.

Liberty folded, and I secretly rejoiced, but then I was given two publications to sell--the *Saturday Evening Post* and *Ladies Home Journal.* I was told how excited people would be to buy them and how fortunate I was to have the opportunity to sell these prestigious magazines. What first struck me, however, was the added weight in my bike basket. The bike was a Western Flyer from the Western Auto Store in St. Paul, and it looked a lot like a Schwinn but cost half as much.

They loaded me up, and since I was conscientious, I felt I had to keep selling until those magazines were gone--which, I came to realize, was exactly what they had in mind. I was learning, after all.

I didn't fully understand that my best prospects for the *Ladies Home Journal* were women so I approached women and men alike saying only, "*Journal*?" After trying unsuccessfully to sell the *Journal* to men at Smith Welding, the Pillsbury flour mill and White Motor Company, I caught on.

Although I did not become truly successful, I did develop a loyal number of women who were ready and eager to receive the *Journal* when I came calling. The woman on Malcom Avenue often wore a print dress with big tulips on it, and each month I could report to Mom that the tulip lady had bought again. As a bonus, she usually gave me a cookie. Some women asked about my family and what grade I was in and even if I had a girlfriend. That made me feel good, but not quite as good as I felt when I was playing ball.

The *Saturday Evening Post* was different. My circulation manager heaped magazines on me beyond my capacity to sell so I not only made the rounds of residential neighborhoods, but also canvassed more businesses on University Avenue.

There were factories and distributorships and various light industries that smelled of metal shavings, glue, apple pies or rubber. I found that if I avoided the front office ("Whatever you're selling, we don't want any!") I could sneak in the back or side door and approach workers at their stations. Mostly they said no. I even practiced looking forlorn.

At the Paramount Pie factory, the man who kneaded dough by slapping it alternately against the wall and then his belly, was always good for a sale. He was kindly and had a twinkle in his eye. If I had earned enough from my route that month, I'd stop by the factory and buy a half-priced pie just to show my support and loyalty to my friend with the big belly.

During summer, our family would travel to Lake Michigan and the Upper Peninsula town of Gladstone, where Dad was born and raised. We'd travel in our REO Flying Cloud--"America's Finest Six." It was a 1936 model--the last year REO made cars, and it was Dad's pride and joy.

Under Dad's tutelage, I learned to log roll. There in the Gladstone yacht basin I spent my days learning the art of snubbing and cuffing and reversing on the log, all in preparation for the yearly competition. Dad would stand hip-deep in water, puffing on his cigar and shouting encouragement as I strained to stay on top of the fast-turning log.

My hard work paid off, and in 1941 I won the World's Junior Log Rolling Championship. I was quietly proud to wear my new jacket with the World Championship design on the back when I walked into town for a black raspberry cone at the little ice cream shop on Delta Avenue.

When I got back to Minneapolis, I still had to sell magazines. But a couple of months after the Michigan trip, we got word that the *Post* was going to carry an article on the log rolling championships. Dad was ecstatic, and it was an exciting day when my copies of the September 27, 1941 issue of the *Saturday Evening Post* came and--wow--the article named me as junior log rolling champion.

Dad ordered lots of extra copies. Besides being proud of me, he thought I would be able make extra money by selling lots of magazines. He sent me out with the admonition, "Don't hide your light under a bushel, boy." Until I was 40, I thought Dad originated that line.

Unfortunately, Dad didn't factor in my shyness. My one-word sales pitch, "*Post*?" stretched to four, "*Post*? I'm in it." I spoke so softly that, without further explanation, I was largely unheard or misunderstood.

It didn't matter. Dad happily bought all my leftover copies and gave them proudly to his friends, neighbors, office mates or anyone who would listen or look. It relieved my shame of not having sold them and made me feel really good about Dad's pride.

While I settled into a routine of selling each month's allotment of magazines, I never really learned to enjoy the job. Nevertheless, it taught me some valuable lessons about money, goals, work and most importantly, people. Selling magazines may have made me a better ad man, my eventual profession. In fact, it may have made me a better person. Not a bad trade off.

Young Ted Springer on his Western Flyer

South Minneapolis native Ted Springer worked for B.B.D.O. advertising for more than thirty years. After retirement he taught skiing in Vail, Colorado

Before the Fall
by Myrna C.G. Mibus

Pride comes before a fall, and when I was a 14-year-old living in Richfield, I learned this lesson from an unlikely teacher, my brother's 1963 Willys Jeep.

It was the summer of 1981. My friends were all out of town, and I was stuck at home. Dad was at work. My little brother Joel was napping, and Mom was in the back yard hanging the wash on the line. I had nothing better to do so I went outside to bother my brother Donnie, who was working on his prized possession, a rather odd-looking, 1963 Willys Jeep.

The Willys was in the driveway, its front tires perched on wooden ramps. All I could see of Donnie were his feet sticking out from underneath his Jeep. Spending time with my brother was not something I really liked doing, but I figured maybe I could get him to do something dumb like wipe oil on his face so I could make fun of him.

"Hi Donnie." I let out an annoyed sounding sigh just to let him know I was not happy to be there.

"Oh, hi," Donnie sounded surprised as he rolled out from under the Jeep on his creeper, oil filter in hand. His face already had oil on it. Darn, I thought. That's the end of my fun for the day

"You here to help me?"

"I suppose," I mumbled, trying not to sound enthusiastic.

"Good enough." He rolled back under his Willys. I sat in the grass, already bored. It wasn't that I didn't like cars. I sort of did. They weren't as interesting as horses, but I liked learning about them, a little. And helping Donnie was one way I could learn a thing or two.

Knowing about cars came in handy in our family. Dad and Donnie were car guys who always wanted to visit car museums or something equally exciting like threshing bees or gas engine shows.

Since Mom enjoyed these things too and Joel was too young to have an opinion, family events usually involved automobiles of some sort. I had learned years before that to get any attention in the family, I either had to cry my eyes out, scream, or act interested in cars.

"Hey Myrna," Donnie called. "Hand me that oil filter wrench."

I shuffled over to his toolbox and picked up the wrench. "Here you go." I didn't always help my brother when he asked. Sometimes I pretended not to hear him. But today I decided to be a good sister, or at least, better than usual and handed him tools while he finished the oil change. Frankly, while I preferred talking about equine horse power instead of engine torque and acceleration speeds, I knew my way around the tool box and looked forward to the day when I too would have my own wheels. Still, I wasn't about to let my brother know that I sort of liked his ugly Jeep. And I certainly wasn't going to get him talking about it because if I did that, I'd be stuck with him all day.

Done with the oil change, Donnie rolled out, wiped his oily hands on his jeans, and dropped the oil wrench in his tool box. "Thanks for helping, Myrn."

"Sure." I tried to look bored, but I was glad I had helped him.

He took his keys from his pocket. " Do you want to back it off the ramps?"

"Ah, sure. I guess so." He handed me the keys.

"Well, just jump right in there, turn the key and start her up." Before he could rethink his offer, I put one foot on the running board and opened the driver's side door and started to climb in. He started giving me instructions, which I needed, but I tuned him out as best I could. I may be his little sister, I thought, but I know a thing or two about cars, and I sure don't need him to tell me what to do.

"Make sure you've got your foot on the clutch and the brake..." his voice droned on as I grabbed the 18-wheeler sized steering wheel and pulled myself in. "...and be sure to put it in reverse while you..."

"I know, Donnie, I know." I rolled my eyes as I settled myself onto the turquoise colored, vinyl covered seat.

"...slowly let out the clutch and press on the accelerator."

"Yeah, Donnie." I bounced in the seat feeling tall, feeling proud that my brother would let me drive his own Jeep. I was pleased that I would be driving, if only down the ramps, while my friends were sitting on the beach, merely getting suntans and picking up boys.

"You know where reverse is now, don't cha Myrna?" I sat up straight, my left foot on the brake, my right on the clutch.

"Yes Donnie," I smiled smugly as I turned the key. "I know." I was ready to drive my brother's Jeep off the ramps. Or so I thought.

At 14, my experiences behind the wheel had been limited to driving with Dad down a gravel road at a farm in Iowa, holding the steering wheel a few times while Dad took off his coat on a straight stretch of highway, and helping my cousin David drive his dad's car into a pond. We were 5 years old at the time. Yet, in my mind, I'd had plenty quality time behind the wheel. I knew I was a beginner, but believed I was a very capable one. There was just one problem, even with all of my experience, I had never driven a vehicle with a stick shift transmission.

My brother must have known of my limited driving experience so I puzzled at why he would let me drive, but I wasn't going to ask him why he was offering me this once in a lifetime chance. Maybe he was excited that I had taken an interest in his Jeep. Or maybe he forgot that I was 14 and really couldn't drive. Then again, perhaps he thought that the family's motor-head genes would enable me to drive without training or practice. Whatever the reason, my brother trusted me, trusted that I could safely put his Jeep in reverse and smoothly back it off the ramps and deliver it onto the driveway. Boy was he wrong.

"Go ahead, Myrna, I'm ready for you." My brother was standing a safe distance away from the Jeep near its rear, ready to tell me when I had backed clear of the wooden ramps. He was ready, but I sure wasn't.

I realized at that moment, with the engine running and my pride overflowing, that I only had a vague idea of where the reverse gear was. I was pretty sure it was somewhere to the left side of the shifting pattern. I looked at the gear lever, hoping to see a shifting diagram on the knob like I'd seen in other cars. But the round, metal, stick-shift knob didn't offer any guidance.

I remembered there was a yellow and black shifting diagram inside the glove box. Yes, I could picture it exactly. But since I had the engine running and could see my brother gesturing for me to get it moving, I decided I wouldn't waste my time actually looking at that diagram. I was sure, or sure enough, that reverse gear was "stick left and back."

With all my might, I confidently shoved the metal lever as far left as it would go, then pulled it towards me with authority, all the time thinking how wonderful I was, how Donnie would be pleased with my skills, how I could drive his Jeep and back it off the ramps like a pro.

"All right, Donnie. Here I come." I smiled as I eased my foot off the brake and clutch and smoothly pressed the accelerator. All at once, the Jeep lurched forward, and the engine quit. I heard a remarkable BANG as the Willys landed with a thud. All was silent except for the slight creaking of the seat spring and the beating of my heart.

My mother came running from the back yard, clothespins in one hand, clean underwear, shirts and socks in her arms. Donnie stood with his mouth open, staring at the sight before him. I sat dumbfounded, mouth agape, in the driver's seat. My legs were shaking as I held the shift lever in one hand and gripped the steering wheel in the other.

Donnie was walking around the Jeep, busily inspecting his precious baby. Mom stood at the driver's door and looked at me, silent, her mouth a thin line, her eyes as big as the Jeep's steering wheel. I was sure I was going to get yelled at for being so stupid, for driving off the ramps, for almost wrecking my brother's Jeep.

Inspection complete, Donnie walked over to Mom and announced, "She didn't hurt a thing, Mom. Look, she just drove it off the front of the ramps." Mom leaned over to inspect the running boards and the fenders.

The Jeep sat patiently, waiting for someone to pull the ramps out from under her. I sat in fear, waiting for my brother to yell, waiting for my mom to tell me I would never drive again. "Are you okay?" Mom asked me through the window.

"Yeah." I said quietly, legs still shaking, tears ready to flow. Oh, why didn't I just look at the shifting diagram? Why didn't I ask Donnie for directions? I wondered as I got ready to beg for forgiveness.

But before I could tell my mom and brother how sorry I was, before I could promise that I would find out where reverse was before I shifted next time, before I could plead for a chance to ever drive again, Mom and Donnie started laughing. I breathed a sigh. I was forgiven.

I heard them talking as they walked into the house, about how they couldn't wait to tell Dad what I did. About how I didn't ask where reverse was and about how they'd never seen anyone drive a Jeep, or anything else for that matter, off ramps that way. And since I learned my lesson, they would never see it happen again.

The Willys Jeep today

Myrna CG Mibus grew up in Richfield and lives in Webster. Her favorite hobby is flying her vintage airplane with her husband and two children. Her email address is myrnacgmibus@mac.com

Brake Stands
by Myrna C.G. Mibus

When I was 18, my favorite cousin David visited my family for a few days. We were the same age and generally could come up with some kind of trouble to get into--like the time we drove his father's car. We were about 5 years old at the time, and we wouldn't have gotten caught if it weren't for the tree that was in our way. This time, however, we were hard pressed to come up with anything to do. Finally, David and I decided to drive my 1976 Sunbird coupe around town to pass the time. We were bored within minutes. Then David had an idea that was sure to cure our boredom.

"Hey, let's do some brake stands, Myrna. They're fun." I had no idea what a brake stand was, but I worshipped my cousin and couldn't imagine saying no to anything he suggested. I looked at him in awe as he explained the procedure. "Put your left foot on the Sunbird's brake," he instructed.

"Done. Now what?" I asked

"Now put your right foot on the accelerator, all the way to the floor." The engine raced as I firmly pressed on the accelerator pedal. "Okay, Myrna, when I tell you, take your foot off the brake and we'll see how long a skid mark this Sunbird can leave."

"Okay, David." My hands gripped the wheel. I looked straight ahead. I pumped the accelerator to rev the engine. I looked, I was sure, like a NASCAR driver. I looked at David and nodded, "I'm ready."

"Now!" David yelled. My foot leaped off the brake.

"Whoa!" I screamed, as the power of six cylinders pushed me back in my seat, and the smell of burned rubber wafted through our windows. "This is fun!" I slowed the Sunbird to a stop and David jumped out to look at the skid marks we left on the once-quiet streets of Richfield.

"Yeah! All right. You did great!" David's eyes were bright with excitement as he climbed back into my car. "Let's do it again."

So we did--several times. I suspected squealing tires might not be the best thing for my car but I didn't care. I was having fun. Besides, I figured, this newfound skill might come in handy some day. Well, maybe not. But at least I could do something that my other friends couldn't. "I am so cool!" I told myself as I drove home to tell someone about my new driving technique.

We pulled into the driveway and saw my dad working in the garage, and he wasn't my first choice of a person to talk to. But David dashed into the house to find my brother, and as I sat behind the wheel, engine still running, a strange thought flashed through my mind. Tell Dad about doing brake stands? No, I thought, what a silly idea. Dad wouldn't want to hear about this; he hardly even likes me. But then I remembered how often Dad talked to my brother about cars, and I felt a little sad that I didn't talk to him very often. Maybe I could tell him about doing brake stands and we could do a little father daughter bonding.

I took my keys out of the ignition, got out of my Sunbird, shut the door and walked to the garage and Dad. For a moment, I thought about diving into the house unnoticed and forgetting the whole idea. What am I thinking? I can't talk to him. Then, oh, come on, Myrna, be a good daughter and talk to the guy. After all, Dad was the only person around, and I was bubbling over with excitement about "burning rubber."

I walked into the garage. It was dark and cool, smelling faintly of oil and WD-40. Dad stood over an old garbage disposal motor he had clamped into the workbench vise. He was pulling coils of copper wire out of the motor with a needle nose pliers, methodically putting the copper into a bucket to take to the recycling center. He spent long hours recycling metal from all sorts of things he found lying around. To say he was thrifty was an understatement.

Guess what, Dad? " He looked up. His eyes squinted as he tried to see me against the light from the open garage door.

"Oh, it's you. What, Myrna?"

I wanted to say, "Of course it's me. What other girl comes in and says, 'Guess what, Dad?'" But I remembered I was trying to be a nice daughter so I said, "David taught me how to do brake stands in the Sunbird. I made skid marks all over."

Dad's eyebrows raised, his hand holding the pliers stopped in mid air above his workbench. "Brake stands. Hmm. You know that's not real good for the car, don't you?"

"Uh, no. I just thought it was something you do, for fun." Since when did Dad know how to have fun? He was the most un-fun guy I knew. All work and no play. Making hay while the sun shines. Up at dawn and working until nightfall. He didn't watch TV. He couldn't sit still for a moment without falling asleep. Why on earth did I tell him?

But, instead of telling me how brake stands and squealing tires caused undue wear on the tires and engine, he looked me in the eye and asked, "How long were the skid marks?"

Was he trying to catch me at something? Was I going to get in trouble for ruining the tires? Would he charge me a fine based on the length of the skid marks? Could I pretend I didn't hear his question and run into the house?

Dad was peering at me over his glasses, waiting, so I had no choice but to answer. "Oh, five to ten feet long, I suppose," I said as I concentrated my gaze on the clock on the wall. I was afraid I would see Dad's blue eyes flashing, his temper exploding like the time when Donnie and David ran over a rake with the farm truck. Or when we were on vacation in Colorado and the car overheated and Dad got out and kicked the tire, jumped up and down and yelled at the top of his lungs while everyone driving by stared.

"Hmm. That's pretty good." He actually looked somewhat pleased. I was bewildered, Dad wasn't mad. He wasn't going to yell. He seemed almost proud of me. I looked up at him and saw just a glimmer of a smile and a faraway look in his eyes, as if he were thinking of something from long before he had three children and a mortgage and a job fixing other people's broken stuff.

"Yep, that's pretty good." He nodded slowly. "You know, once, in my '56 Pontiac Starchief convertible, I laid skid marks over 20 feet long."

What? My Dad, drove around making skid marks? Having fun? No, it couldn't be true. Not my boring, hard working, thrifty father who was taking a half hour to recycle copper wire that was worth 40 cents. "Really?" I said tentatively. "When did you do that?"

He sighed a long sigh and started pulling copper wire again. "Oh, years ago, before your mom and I were married. A long time ago."

"Sounds like..." Did I dare say it? "Sounds like fun, Dad."

He looked up once again and smiled a tired smile. "It was." He went back to work. As I walked to the house he said, "Just don't have too much fun with that little car of yours or you'll wear out the tires."

"Yeah, Dad, okay." I opened the screen door. In the moment before I let it slam behind me, I looked at my father and imagined him as a young man screeching around town in his Pontiac, smiling from ear to ear--having fun. I blinked and saw him again, just as I had left him, busy at work, head bent over his workbench, pulling copper wire.

The Sunbird

The Forever Baby
by Lorna Rafness

My maternal grandmother, Jona (Sigurjona Eyjolfsdottir), was born in Iceland in 1878. She was 2 years old and her sister Gudmunda was a babe in arms when the family immigrated to Minneota, where her grandparents and other Icelanders had homesteaded.

Soon after arriving in their new country, Jona's father was kicked by a workhorse. At first the extent of his injuries wasn't realized, but several days later he died. At the time a young Icelander by the name of Jon Snidal lived with them and worked for the family. Whether out of convenience, propriety, or affection, within the year the widowed mother and Jon Snidal were joined in wedlock. Jona and Munda became Snidals, along with their seven yet to be born half-brothers and sisters.

This small community of newcomers willfully retained their native language and exclusivity into the next generation. Within her world of family, housework and farm work, Jona was secure in her sense of belonging. As the oldest and a girl, she had to work hard indoors and outdoors. One diversion from work was to attend church services in private homes. When Jona could be spared, she attended school, also held in settlers' homes, until she was 13. Jona spoke only Icelandic until her own children brought the new language home from school. From them she learned to speak English and to write enough to get by.

The man who became her husband, Olafur Rafnson, had left Iceland when he was 17 to join relatives in the farm community of Minneota. In 1899, 30 years old and sporting a black handlebar mustache, he ventured to speak for the hand of his diminutive neighbor girl, Sigurjona. She was 21 and knew little of life beyond her farmstead when she agreed to wed the gentle farmer.

The land they rented, not far from their parents, was a world away in Jona's mind. Work horses, wagons and rutted country roads didn't facilitate travel, but Jona had always understood that work was the way of life. That was just the way things were. Irrelevant to her were the words or thoughts of pleasure; that was all foolishness.

Jona was 22 when she gave birth to her first child in 1900, and two years later a second girl was born. Although the labor of survival weighed heavily on the young couple, the healthy babies gladdened their lives. And in April of 1904, yet another girl, Runa, christened Gudrun, was born. Little Runa wasn't like their first two babies: there was no sparkle in her eyes, she couldn't hold her head up, or smile, or even try to roll over, sit up, or learn to crawl. Ever.

A fourth daughter was born in 1906, followed by their first son in 1908. That made five little ones for Jona to tend while they eked out a living from the raw land. On that farm there were no labor-saving machines and in that farmhouse no conveniences: no hot water, no indoor plumbing, no electricity, no telephone.

Four of the children were robust, thriving youngsters, but Runa remained a helpless infant. Growing some, but not flourishing, she did not become a laughing little girl. She was not to be a raven-haired beauty like her sisters. At age 6, weighing less than 30 pounds, she could not sit up, walk, talk or feed herself. She cried incessantly, but Jona, with her multitude of obligations, was devoted to Runa, her forever-baby.

Midmorning on November 15, 1910, Doc Thor drove up in his Model T. Both Jona and Olaf were taken aback. Visitors were rare, few people they knew owned a motorcar, and a social call from the busy doctor was unheard of.

Only a month earlier another child had been born. The doctor hadn't been called because they couldn't pay him. But he had heard about the birth, and he had come to examine the mother and newborn. Jona's recovery was painfully slow. It was all she could do to take care of the baby and Runa.

Why was the doctor calling again so soon? Over cups of black coffee several topics were discussed before the revered doctor could bring himself to say what he had come to say. In the midst of tending to Runa's cries, Jona listened as the doctor bluntly stated to Olaf, "You have to make a choice right now." And pointing first to Runa and then to Jona he said, "Either the girl must go or you will lose the mother."

Just after the noon hour, on that very day, the doctor drove the father and small daughter across the state to the School for the Feeble Minded, later known as the Faribault State Hospital. Jona never saw Runa again. She had been diagnosed as a victim of marasmus, a condition of progressive emaciation due to an inability to assimilate food. It was a shame and not to be talked about, the baby who wasn't right—but the greatest shame was to give your baby away. Over the years Olaf made the journey alone two or three times to see his daughter before she died and was buried at the State Hospital in her twelfth year.

Jona told her daughter Joann, and Joann told me, how she had faced the truth and had given up. The burden had become too heavy. How long could she have persevered caring for the helpless little creature, in addition to the other children, and the new babies that were sure to come? Her strength was only that of one human being.

After Runa was taken from her, it was another fourteen years before Jona set foot off the farm. She told Joann that after that day she was never the same. Her sense of justice and her belief in the order of the universe were shattered.

Helping Grandma
by Lorna Rafness

Our family routinely visited my paternal grandparents on their farm seven miles north of Minneota. They were of Norwegian ancestry and lived extremely orderly lives with a place for everything and everything in its place.

Sometimes one or two or all three of us girls would stay with Grandpa Otto and Grandma Josie for a few days. We liked staying there, but my middle sister Midge always got homesick and either developed a hemorrhagic bloody nose or got sick to her stomach and threw up. Then she wouldn't quit crying until one of our parents came to get her or until Grandpa drove her home. That was always in the middle of the night, but she was so cute the adults all liked her anyway.

At the farm we were supposed to be helping Grandma by picking eggs, feeding the chickens, cleaning house and running errands. I don't think we were much help inside or outside. Mama never made me work at home so I didn't know much about housework. I guess that's why I had to be the egg picker.

There was nothing likable about those chickens. They were downright hostile when you took their eggs, but I was no coward. Grandma Josie gave me a bucket to put the eggs in and carry back to the house. I'd go out and force myself to go into the chicken coop all alone.

Once inside I'd stand there adjusting my eyes to the darkness and trying to build up my courage. Reaching out my hand and looking the hen in the eye, I wavered every time. Maybe she wouldn't peck at my fingers, but maybe she would. I told myself I was the boss and I was bigger.

I tried, but I just couldn't reach under the hens for their eggs. I'd look around for a small board or a big stick and push them off their nests so I could get the eggs. I didn't hit them or hurt them, I just pushed them off. That worked pretty well, and there were always a few henless nests with an egg just waiting to be picked.

I remember the last time I picked eggs. When I was on my way to the house with the bucket of eggs, I realized something strange was happening. The chickens were following me, and all of a sudden I was surrounded by them. I began to feel afraid. Their low ominous clucking was aimed directly at me. It seemed like they were going to attack me. I thought they must want their eggs back, and in my panic I threw an egg into their midst.

Those chickens went crazy, all of them diving after the broken egg, cackling maniacally. That worked so well to distract them that I threw another egg. Frenzied, they carried on like that every time I threw an egg.

All the commotion got Grandpa Otto's attention, and in no time he appeared there at the scene of the crime. He didn't look real mad, but I knew I'd done the wrong thing. He told me I shouldn't have done that because Grandma needed the eggs, and I'd better go and tell her what I did.

"Oh no," I thought but didn't say anything. I'd rather die than have to tell Grandma I'd been bad. I wasn't 8 years old yet, and already I was a criminal. Grandpa didn't ask me why I threw the eggs, and I didn't try to tell him. I just hung my head and trudged to the house to face Grandma.

As soon as I saw her I started crying, and in between gasping sobs I told her that I threw some of her eggs at the chickens. Her response was to shush me and pet me and give me cookies saying, "There, there, don't cry. It's all right…you didn't mean to," always on the verge of tears herself if someone else felt bad.

Minneota native Lorna Rafness lives in Mankato, where she and her husband work as writers. The mother of two daughters, she has a masters degree in sociology and is retired from a 32-year postal career.

Remembrances of Childhood in Minneota
by Lorna Rafness

My sisters and I enjoyed Grandma Josie's baking day. If we weren't too greedy, she allowed us to eat snatches of raw dough while we helped her. Doughnuts were our favorites. She told us we would get worms from eating raw dough, but we didn't believe it. She spoke too kindly to make it sound alarming, and like my dad, she couldn't say no to us. Sometimes for breakfast she'd give us a big slice of her fresh homemade bread on a plate with thick cream and brown sugar on it. We loved it.

When we stayed overnight, we slept in the living room on the davenport, a couch that made into a double bed. If it happened to be all three of us girls, we nestled in spoon-style for the night.

Their small farmhouse was sparsely and functionally furnished. Besides the davenport in that room, they had two sturdy wooden rocking chairs, his and hers; his was bigger with a higher back. There was a library table, a roll-top desk, and a small table with a radio on it. The radio was the focal point of the room the way televisions are now. Those pieces were lined up around the room except for Grandma's rocker. It sat out in the room and faced the radio. With her back to the rest of the room, she rocked and listened. She did embroidery but never seemed to finish it.

Bedtime came early, shortly after dark, with everyone going to bed at the same time. Their early-to-bed routine didn't change even after they got electricity when I was 6 or 7 years old. Grandma always had us say our prayers for her before we snuggled down for the long night. That would mean reciting "The Lord's Prayer" and any other prayers we could think of. Grandma approved of long prayers, and we liked to please Grandma.

Those nights at their house seemed endless, partly because we went to bed so early and partly because they got up many times during the night. One or both would get up and sit, quietly rocking. Sometimes the radio would be turned on very low. Their only conversation would be in whispered Norwegian. They might have hot milk or a snack or a peppermint, but we knew we should just be quiet and go back to sleep.

Their small bedroom with only a bed, dresser, and one wooden chair was just off the living room. The kitchen seemed large with its wood-burning cook stove, a big round oak table and chairs, and one freestanding cupboard holding all their dishware and cooking necessities.

Off the kitchen was a large pantry with the cream separator sitting right in the middle of the room. I can still taste the warm milk separated from the cream that was the product of that big machine. Grandpa had a few cows he milked by hand. When he quit milking, the separator disappeared, and the pantry became their first indoor bathroom. Before I was in my teens, about 1952, Grandpa had given up all his livestock and rented out a good share of his land.

The upstairs had a large hallway with Grandma's huge trunk in it, and there were three small bedrooms. One was used as a storage room, and one was a mixed storage/bedroom. I don't remember being told we couldn't play upstairs, but for some reason we rarely did. Maybe it was because the stairway was dark and angled with slippery, narrow wooden steps. The entire house had slippery hardwood floors.

Grandpa, always the naysayer, worried we would hurt ourselves or break something as we played. At home one of our favorite places to play was in the hayloft, but Grandpa wouldn't allow it on his farm unless my dad was there. Dad would scoff at Grandpa saying, "Those little girls aren't going to hurt anything, and they aren't going to get hurt. Let 'em play wherever they want." Always, there was tension between the two of them.

To Grandpa we were an annoyance, but Grandma wanted us nearby because she liked us. It was hard for her to go up and down the steps so she had us sleep downstairs, keeping us close to her while we slept, to pet us and keep us tucked in during the night.

On rare occasions she invited us upstairs with her to look through the treasures she kept in the trunk there. We were both awed and excited to witness her examine each item. There were tiny handmade baby clothes, colorful old silk dresses and hats, fancy gloves, and letters wrapped in ribbon. Most memorable to me were the many elaborate old Valentines she'd saved from years past.

Probably the most endearing thing about my grandpa was that he always wore a flannel nightshirt and nightcap to bed. He had a very handsome but very bald head, and I suppose that was why he needed to wear a nightcap. He was the only person I ever knew who owned a nightcap, much less wore one to bed every night.

Grandpa Otto wasn't always stern and crabby; he just seemed that way because he was so different from our dad. He never did get angry with us, never more than the mildest scolding. It was the potential for anger his attitude conveyed that made me cautious around him. He had a funny snickering kind of laugh, like he was trying to hold it in, not unpleasant, but suppressed. When he did laugh or joke, it was extra-special coming from him, and he had an endless supply of white or pink round fat peppermints for us. He required order in his life, and while Grandma enjoyed us all of the time, I know he enjoyed us some of the time. They were good and kind people, but paramount was the unfailing care and respect they had for each other.

I was 7 when we moved to town, and our parents convinced us that Sandy, our big dog, would be happier on a farm. Grandpa Otto and Grandma Josie were glad to give Sandy a home. When my pure white cat Tuffy developed a swelling on one side of his face that turned into an open sore, we had to give Tuffy to Grandpa and Grandma too.

Kerr's Chicken Hatchery was a thriving business in Minneota, and they employed Japanese specialists to cull out the roosters from the hens. The roosters were disposed of, and I heard Kerr's gave them to kids if they came in and asked for baby chicks. Because I loved animals, I went right down and asked for some. That's how I acquired two of the little yellow peepers, confident that my mother would like them too. She did, as long as I agreed to leave them in the barn at night. There was a ramshackle barn and corral behind our house, and they were safe there in a cardboard box.

Baby chicks were way more likable than Grandma's nasty hens. Most days I would play with them in the yard and sometimes leave them by the back door under the dense and leafy foliage plants that grew around the house. They liked scratching around for bugs and seeds in their own private jungle.

A heavy rain and hail storm came up one day when I had left them outside. It was after they lost their yellow fluff and had acquired white feathers. I forgot about them when the storm began, but when big hailstones hit the windows, I remembered they were outside alone. I made a mad dash to save them, but I wasn't fast enough. One of them got hit on the head by a big hailstone. It made him goofy, hopping and flopping around for the rest of the day before he died.

The other rooster, Elmer, fared better through the storm and grew up to follow me around the rest of that summer. By late fall though, he started chasing people, anyone who came into our back yard, flying at them and trying to peck them, everyone but me. So my pet rooster had to go to Grandpa's farm. Even my dad, who was always on my side, agreed that Elmer had to go. For a long time I could pick him out of the crowd of other poultry at Grandpa's, but gradually I lost track of him. They never told me, but I suspected later that Elmer ended up being chicken soup.

We moved to Minneota in the summer, and it was the following spring when each of us girls became the owner of a lamb. My dad had started a trucking business, and through his wheeling and dealing ended up bringing three white lambs home to us. The old barn and broken-down corral in our backyard was a perfect place to raise them.

We bottle-fed them for awhile, and my lamb Fluffy and I fell in love with each other. My sisters were more interested in other things and didn't pay much attention to their lambs. But everyday I fed and petted and combed my lamb, and when I let Fluffy out of the corral, she followed me everywhere I went. She really did, all around the neighborhood, until I led her back to the barn. However, after school started, I got busy with other things and paid less and less attention to Fluffy. By the time they were big enough to sell, the charm of the cute little lambs had worn off. Then it didn't take too much to convince me that someone else would take better care of Fluffy than I could.

I wished Grandpa would take her like he did all our other pets, but my dad said he couldn't. I wasn't told what would become of Fluffy, but I guessed she'd go to live on a farm. So none of us objected when all three of them disappeared one day while we were in school. And some days later we each got a savings account book with $100 in it. I felt bad for awhile when I realized I'd traded in my pet for a savings account. But the truth was that I had fallen out of love with Fluffy the lamb when she turned into a sheep.

For about three years, between the ages of 5 and 7, I got to help alongside my sisters with the fieldwork at Grandpa's. It was only for a few days each summer. We picked mustard out of the wheat, oats, or flax and we chopped down the cockleburs. We were never overworked and my labor was too much fun to be very productive.

I only got in on a couple harvest seasons before Grandpa rented his land out. The most fun was when we took lunch out to the field. They started work so early in the morning that the men were famished by 10. It was energizing to be part of the hustle and bustle—the men working together, hard and fast—and Grandma in the kitchen conjuring up rewards for their labor, her own labor rewarded by their ravenous appetites.

Grandma had a hand-operated metal coffee grinder attached to the pantry wall. Other people I knew bought their coffee already ground, but she used coffee beans she ground herself, eliciting a rich aroma that stirred my senses. She poured fresh-brewed, boiling hot coffee into Mason jars, screwed the lids on tight, and wrapped the jars in clean white dish towels. She wrapped in waxed paper roast beef sandwiches on her homemade brown bread spread with sweet butter. Cream and sugar for the coffee and both dill pickles and sweet pantry pickles were included, along with chocolate-frosted chocolate cake and utensils, all to be transported in baskets to the field. We, the lunch bearers with piqued appetites, got to eat with the workers. They let me drink coffee with cream and sugar in it, and it was the best coffee and lunch I ever tasted.

That was midmorning lunch break. At harvest-time with extra help, some neighbors and some hired, they had to come to the house for the big noon meal that might consist of fried chicken, mashed potatoes and gravy, corn, cucumbers and onions in mayonnaise sauce, pickled beets, more homemade bread and butter, and for sure, pie for desert.

I don't remember Grandma doing the work she must have done. It must be that children don't recognize adult domestic labor. The clean house and good food seemingly materialized without effort.

Only two images of her at work come to my mind. In one, wearing a bibbed apron over her house dress, she is outside scattering feed to the chickens. In another, as always in her clean-bibbed apron, she is rolling out doughnut dough. Behind her, on the cook stove, melted fat is bubbling up in a heavy pot.

She was rarely disheveled, but in this image she has a streak of flour across her nose and one cheek. As she shapes and rolls the dough with her big wooden rolling pin, she lets us each take a turn pressing the metal mold into the dough. Then we watch, anxious to see that we get the right one back, as she fries our doughnuts.

I don't leave my doughnut while it cools. I inhale its fresh aroma and then blow on it—savoring the thought of how it's going to taste, crispy on the outside and then melting in my mouth. I saved up the fried doughnut holes, as many as I could finagle, rolling them around on the table or stacking them in a pyramid before I ate them.

When it wasn't planting or harvest season, my grandparents' life was easier, and the long winters were peaceful and quiet on the farm. They routinely rose early and had a breakfast of coffee and oatmeal or her homemade bread with cream and brown sugar on it. Midmorning was coffee-time with a doughnut or a cookie, or a piece of cake or pie. Then it was their noon meal, scaled down but still called dinner.

At mid-afternoon it was coffee-time again. Supper was a light meal of leftovers at 6 o'clock sharp. And then there was always a little something before bedtime. Food never tasted as good anywhere else.

My most vivid memories of them and their life was after their hardest work years were over. After they rented out their land and sold off the livestock, their labors were of their own choosing. Still, they always kept to their routine of early to bed, early to rise, and still had their many punctually appointed repasts.

As you might guess, Grandma Josie was roly-poly, ample-bosomed, short and plump, whereas the descriptive word for Grandpa Otto was solid. A stoic Norwegian, about 5'8," he was neither fat nor stocky, but solid—in character as well as physique.

It seems like time stood pleasantly still at the farm, with long dreamy nights and slow easygoing days. Their relaxed, folksy ways gave that appearance, but their life was never lazy, never idle. They moved at their own measured pace so unlike the frantic rush this modern world demands.

Steeped in nostalgic longing for what once was, I'm guilty of romanticizing the past. But acknowledging that I can't back up time or stop so-called progress, I've become a selective Luddite. For example, I like using this word processor, but I detest the technology that allows telemarketers to jangle my nerves with their uninvited calls. I try to get along in this high tech era by taking the time to make thoughtful choices and to take control of what is in my power to control. For years I've been making a conscious effort to fashion a lifestyle more like my grandparents—to piece together the better part of both worlds to build a good life.

The Severson Sisters: Shirley, Lorna and Midge

Locking Horns With Bullwinkle on the Gunflint Trail
by Ken Nelson

He was bad, he was bold, he was black, he was big--bigger than me--like six times bigger than me, and very likely beautiful to a cow moose. He carried aloft a set of antlers that could easily toss me into the Promised Land.

We met on the coldest morning I had ever experienced in my thirty-odd seasons spent in search of deer. The day began with a strategy assignment, not unusual for me, to take the longest outside route of the morning's drive. I decided to move south from the Gunflint to the old abandoned railroad bed, and then keeping that open space in sight, move until Lima Mountain Lookout was on my right. Then I would zigzag back in the direction of the Gunflint, making sure that I had pushed the area around Locket Lake. I had been in part of this area before, but Locket Lake was new ground to be explored.

I compassed my way in the direction of Locket, and had gone only a hundred yards or so when a big deer jumped close in front of me. Carrying my light caliber .25 Remington Automatic, I touched off a shot and saw a small tree take the bullet between the running deer and me. From the echo of this one shot, the deer turned and came back toward me for what would have been an easy opportunity to harvest a quantity of venison. But my gun misfired.

I'm certain the well-below-zero temperature of that morning had gripped the automatic mechanism and prompted the malfunction. Repeated efforts to rechamber new rounds brought the same result. The deer disappeared into the woods as I stood trying to figure out the problem.

Moving deeper into the forest with a gun of questionable ability to function, I crested a rise in the terrain that opened to a stadium-sized arena--complete with tree occupied bleachers and a contained football-field-sized lower level playing field. The playing field portion was for the most part covered with one-inch diameter new-growth trees about eight to ten feet high. As I came down the long slope to that playing field, I discovered a four to five-foot trail leading straight through the middle.

As if standing under one set of goal posts, I looked down that path to where the opposite goal posts one hundred yards away would have been. There standing against the white snow was a very black something, and when that black something turned, I knew at once it was a moose. He immediately trotted toward me to about the fifty-yard point, stopped, and shook his horns very menacingly. At this point my thoughts were focused on finding a tree large enough to separate us if he continued his advance because I knew I was trespassing in his backyard. I stood in the middle of the rut, carrying a firearm that might not respond if I needed to put him down.

Those thoughts were still developing when the moose began a slow and deliberate stalking pace straight down the middle of the path we now shared. When he closed the gap to about thirty yards, I began yelling all sorts of threats at him, but he seemed intent on continuing his challenge. At about ten yards I raised my rifle and hollered, "Stop! Stop! Stop!"

Indeed he did stop. For what seemed like hours but was actually about thirty minutes, we stood locked in eye-to-eye combat. His two widespread nostrils were exhausting vapor trails in the cold air, and my entire body was turning limp.

"My God, he's going away," I thought as he turned broadside. But then he began to shake his massive antlers that towered well above me, even though we stood on level ground. After he stayed in that position for only a couple of minutes, I was a bit relieved when he turned to move away. He took only a couple of steps, however, before he stopped once more to look back. I can only assume he was pondering the wisdom of giving up this challenge.

Slowly he strolled away, knocking over a lot of the small trees in his path, and I beat a slow retreat on wobbly legs, as straight as I could on the Gunflint Trail. I arrived well after the gang had gone back to the lodge for lunch because I plopped down in a snow bank beside the trail. Because of the extreme cold and a body dripping with perspiration, I was lucky when the sheriff of Cook County came around on patrol, picked me up, and took me back to the lodge.

The sheriff was a friend I had hunted and built log cabins with. After stating that I didn't look too good he asked what happened. After I unfolded my story, he advised that I should have put that moose down well before he got that close to me. He told me about two boys who had been treed by a moose a few days earlier, and about a moose that had smashed a car's radiator on the Gunflint Trail only a short distance from where he had picked me up. I really needed that information to calm my nerves.

Back at camp, I found the gang had already gone elsewhere for their afternoon hunt, but I was in absolutely no mood to reenter even familiar surroundings. Instead I laid my damp and tired body down on the bed and tried to put my shattered nerves back together. Some time after dropping off to a late afternoon nap, and after the gang had returned and assembled in the dining and living area of our cabin, I had a nightmare to top all nightmares. That same moose, with its massive, towering antlers, crashed through the wall of the bedroom and landed on top of me. I bolted upright and ran from the room yelling all sorts of crazy things. I was greeted by the gang and some concern, but mostly laughter.

After I related the vivid details of my morning adventures, my cousin Ray Nelson, who was near Locket Lake during my standoff with Bullwinkle, indicated that he had heard most of the yelling and had pondered moving to investigate. But he didn't.

A young Ken Nelson, second from left, with an earlier moose, 1946.

Hit by Lightning
by Ken Nelson

As far back as summertime outdoor memories take me, I always enjoyed helping Mom in her big and well-kept garden. Eating strawberries, raspberries, peas, carrots, new onions, rhubarb and especially the tomatoes that didn't need to be wiped on a pant leg helped Mom a lot, because she didn't need to carry my harvested portion into the house. I believe, in hindsight, it also kept me very healthy.

In the mid '50s, after acquiring the additional lot north of the one where we built our home, I relished the thought of turning it mostly into a garden. Planting that garden one day, I was typically sweaty and soiled when a nasty thunder and lightning storm rolled over, driving me inside.

Deciding it was time for my own shower, I hopped in. After lathering up I was at the point where I needed a rinse. Luckily I had my hands off the metal faucets and turned into the full flow of water when a huge bolt of lightning struck our power pole.

The charge rolled into the house, where it finished off two TV sets and a couple of radios. It also jumped into the plumbing and flashed from the shower head to the floor drain. Had I still been holding the metal faucets, I would have been the conductor to ground, and the resulting shock would have been infinitely greater than it was.

The flash that occurred in the conical spray of water that surrounded me and conducted the charge to the ground was brighter than any flashbulb I have ever seen, and the clap on the top of my head felt like a powerfully swung 2 x 4. I staggered from the shower and embraced the thunder mug for a long, long time attempting to catch my breath, which had been knocked out of order.

A week later, when I could still hardly get my head off the pillow to get myself to work, I finally went to see Dr. Nelson, who listened to my story. After giving me some touch tests, he said he believed that the nerve endings in a sizable percentage of my skin had been damaged.

My body was trying to repair itself, and it would likely be several weeks before I would experience full strength again. He was absolutely correct, and I have never taken a shower since when a thunderstorm has been pending. To any and all who may read of this experience--take heed. It was a close call with absolutely no fun involved.

Albert Lea native Ken Nelson worked in engineering, product design, research and sales for Scottsman Industries. He and his wife Vera have three daughters and six grandchildren.

Green Machine Rocket Ride
by Ken Nelson

The day dawned cold--so cold that I walked on lake ice in front of our house, but the forecast was for strong southwest winds and a certainty of record high temperature by day's end. It was December 14, 1998, a day that will live forever in the memories of three generations of the Nelson clan. Granddaughter Sarah was celebrating her 15th birthday on the 17th, and I was going to be 74 on the 18th, a perfect reason to celebrate with a late afternoon party on an unbelievable near-winter day with temps reaching the 70s.

A stroke I experienced in May still had me under Mayo Clinic care, hobbling slowly but without a cane, and gall bladder surgery in late October had my guts still tied up, and the combination of the two caused frequent dizziness.

Because of the extreme winds, we decided to build our hot dog fire in the driveway instead of the lake shore, and amid the hustle and bustle of getting it started, Sarah's birthday wish was to solo on the "Green Machine," a John Deere five-wheel all-materials transport that Lily, their yellow Labrador, loved to bark at. After riding the length of the main driveway several times, Sarah wanted my permission to venture into the south woods. With my okay and a caution about required wide turns, she headed off with Lily in constant pursuit.

With our hot-dog fire lit and needing more fuel, my 9-year-old grandson John and I went to the woodpile for an armload of logs. Just as we came back to the developing fire site, we spotted my daughter Kris racing toward the woods on a dead run.

My first thought was that Lily had nipped once too often at the front wheel and was under the five-wheeler. Expecting the worst, I hobbled toward the woods to see what had taken place. I was met by Kris returning at even a faster pace, out of breath, reporting that the Green Machine was on fire. Quickening my pace from an obvious adrenaline kick, I saw the red glow of flames through the evergreen trees that separated me from the machine that now stood about 100 yards distant.

Kris ran to get fire extinguishers while Sarah and her 13-year-old brother Mark ran to the shed in the woods to get pails to battle the flames with water from the partially frozen frog pond. I arrived at the scene and was amazed to see 18-inch flames completely surrounding the 4-foot square vehicle, and the seat was beginning to burn.

It took only seconds to realize that at any moment the nearly full gas tank was going to explode and create a massive fire that was apt to spread to the tinder-dry trees and ground cover, presenting a severe threat to property and to the young firefighters coming from several directions carrying little more than a bucket with which to battle a gas fire. I quickly determined that the lake where the morning's walkable ice had been fractured by the high warm winds was a tempting and negotiably short 200 feet away. If the engine would start, the best option to divert a crisis was to put the entire machine--fire and all--into that water covered with ice shards.

The Green Machine started on the first compression stroke, and I threw my good leg through the flames now burning the seat. Standing forward of the burning portion, I mashed the throttle and sped forward into the strong west wind. That wind, plus my forward movement, kept flames from igniting the back of my jacket, but about ten feet into the journey, the gas tank exploded and created a whole new set of circumstances.

The explosion altered the straight course I had planned to the lake about 45 degrees, and into rows of 40 or 50-foot-high walnut trees, and the flame trail, according to neighbors who called the Hayward Fire Department, was almost as high as those trees. Something had severed the governor linkage, and I was moving at a much faster speed than was normal for the Green Machine. I somehow managed to slide around a corner just short of hitting the walnut trees as I headed for the lake. In just a matter of seconds, I split through the brush that borders the lake and vaulted into the air off the rocks that protect the fragile shoreline.

The ride at this point was getting very exciting as I prepared to land in the ice shards that the wind had blown in layers along the shoreline. I shut my eyes as I continued a wide-open throttle, hoping the packed ice might propel me into deeper water. I leaned as far back as I could without getting into the fire.

I'm not sure if I prayed, but I must have because when I opened my eyes, the ice shards had slid past my face without any damage, and I was in hip deep water about sixty feet from shore. Now, however, the lake was on fire from the gasoline splashed onto the surface. It was unbelievable that I was stranded in the middle of a circle of fire that was about fifty feet across, with flames that rose at least a foot off the lake.

Prayers--yes--Sarah came from nowhere with a garbage can cover that flew out of the Green Machine when I flew over the rocks. She waded out to the edge of the fire circle and tossed that cover to me. Using the cover as a scoop, I shoveled flames away as I waded toward the wind and out of the fire circle, whereupon I turned and used that cover, with the aid of the wind, to effectively swish most of the flames away from the Green Machine. Kris arrived with fire extinguishers as the few remaining flames exploded the hydraulic system for the box hoist.

Two fire trucks plus a half dozen pickup trucks with Hayward volunteers roared into our yard just as the final flames died out on the lake. To make their run worthwhile, they doused the embers of our hot-dog fire in the driveway. They would not leave, however, until they checked me to make sure I wasn't going to have another stroke from all the excitement.

Badly in need of a hot shower, I suddenly sensed a better command of what had been frequent dizzy spells. The ride back from the icy fire scene did nothing to warm my shivering body, but I didn't seem to be in what had become normal since my stroke--an unbalanced state. Something had changed.

It was also in these moments that I learned that Sarah, Mark and John had used buckets from the woodshed to form a bucket brigade to put out the trail of flames that followed my journey through dry leaves and grass. They very likely prevented a forest fire because just a few feet away from the fire stood hundreds of Christmas tree sized evergreens.

Finally warmed by a welcome shower, I sat at the kitchen table to listen to my wife Vera's version of what had transpired. She told us that the neighbors had suggested she come over to their house until the fire truck arrived. She didn't even know there was a fire.

Our birthday celebration moved inside, where we all assessed the individual moves and decisions made over the past hour or so and determined that some divine guidance had played a big part in the outcome. No one was hurt, including Lily, and no one was burned--except the Green Machine, which we retrieved from the lake a couple of hours later. The next morning the lake froze shut for the winter.

This story does not end there because in a friendly neighborhood chat my daughter Kris had with my gall bladder doctor, she revealed the details of my unexpected rocket ride into the lake. The next week when I went in for a checkup, my doctor asked me to reveal the full story. When I mentioned that my dizziness had improved, the doctor was immediately interested because he had treated me initially when I had my stroke.

A week later, at Mayo Clinic in Rochester for my 6-months stroke recovery assessment, their doctor asked me to relate the full story of my rocket ride into the lake, since it might be worth researching whether or not a magnum adrenaline rush could overcome post stroke dizziness.

My first response was, “How in the world did you hear about that?” to which he responded that it was already in my medical record. In reference to his proposal to conduct research to help future stroke victims I said, “Even if you find this treatment to be successful, I don’t think that you would ever find anyone willing to go through all the steps outlined in the prescription.”

Somewhat worse for wear after recovery from the lake: Green Machine, burned seat and jacket, and garbage pail lid.

Mom's Ordeal
by Clara Graner

One Sunday morning in February of 1925, our mother became very sick. Her pain was so intense that she raced back and forth in the house screaming. Then she threw herself to the floor and got up to run again. Dad called the doctor, and he gave Mom some kind of shot to dull the pain. He said she had gall stones, and he would take her along with him to Wabasha and admit her to St. Elizabeth's Hospital. Since she had a bad cold, the doctor advised no surgery until her cold improved.

After about two weeks shc had the surgery, and at this same time Dad's sister Annie on a farm next door to us was in the final stages of tuberculosis. Both she and Mom were getting progressively worse. Mom had been given the Last Rites of the Church, so when the phone rang on March 11, and a voice told Dad, "Mom died," and then immediately hung up, Dad was not sure if the voice had been that of his niece next door or if it was that of one of my sisters who was in Wabasha at the time.

Dad quickly changed clothes and started for Wabasha, but he stopped next door to check on Aunt Annie's condition. It was then he learned that Aunt Annie, not Mom, had died. Imagine how relieved Dad must have been to know he hadn't lost his wife because he had sixteen children!

Five weeks later, when Mom was finally well, our country roads were in a bad stage of spring breakup. Dad and the doctor decided Mom wouldn't be able to endure riding those rough roads in a buggy for an hour to get home, so Dad contacted Jerry McGraw, the engineer of the little passenger train that always passed by our home at around 11 o'clock each forenoon, and made arrangements for the train to stop ahead of our house and let our mom off.

When the train arrived, Dad was beside the tracks to haul her to the house with horses and wagon, a distance of less than one block. How happy we kids were to have Mom home again!

Clara Graner, age 91, still lives in Wabasha and loves to write about her growing up years. Someone at the Wabasha library encouraged her to submit this story.

The Carson Gang
by Paul Vinck

A reign of terror plagued the streets and neighborhoods on the west side of Albert Lea in the late '40s and early '50s. Every boy I knew between the ages of 5 and 12 lived in mortal fear of the Carson gang, led by a kid with the obvious name of Carson. His first name escapes me because he never had one. He was simply known as Carson, and his two henchmen were the Teff twins, who didn't have first names either.

If they lived in houses like normal kids, I don't know where they were. Except for Carson and the Teffs, the rest of the gang was unfamiliar, unknown. They probably came in from the south side, parts of town so far away they might as well have been in Iowa.

Tales of carnage and mayhem were written on the wind along Fountain Street, Vine Avenue and Lakeview Boulevard.

"Did you hear about Corny Peterson? The Carson gang caught him over on Water Street near the school and beat him to a bloody pulp."

"The Carson gang is getting bigger, and now they're carrying clubs. At least twenty guys cornered Doug Jensen in a garage and poked him till he couldn't stand up. He was so covered with bruises his mother wouldn't let him go outside for a month."

"The Carson gang and those rotten Teff twins are putting rocks in their snowballs, and they're dipping them in water and leaving them outside overnight to freeze solid, and they threw one at Dewey Wilkins and cracked his skull." It seemed like no place was safe from the ravages of these demented gangsters.

Diligence was the order of the day whenever I was outside. I kept a sharp eye focused in all directions in the hope I wouldn't see that dreaded sight--anything that looked like a gang moving toward me. Young boys with a few years of experience on the streets learn how to read such situations. If a bunch of guys are carrying bats and gloves and heading in the general direction of a ball park, they're probably okay. Same was true if they were carrying fishing gear. Bamboo cane poles were too long and unwieldy to be used as weapons. Bicycles were safe also. The Carson gang moved about on foot, and they were not known to ride bikes when on one of their marauding rampages.

At this point, however, I must admit to a point of intellectual honesty. I never actually saw the results of a Carson gang attack. I didn't see with my own eyes Corny Peterson's bloodied face or Doug Jensen's black and blue body or Dewey Wilkins' fractured skull.

Who knows? Maybe Corny only had a bloody nose and Doug a bruise or two. Wilkins may have only had a bump on his allegedly broken head. Who knows how a minor injury might be distorted, magnified and exaggerated in the wide-eyed imaginations of young boys? As the message gets passed along the juvenile grapevine, it is possible that what begins as a nosebleed ends up as bloodletting, a poke or blow becomes paralysis, or a snowball to the forehead sends its target to death's door.

A scholarly research of local news articles of that era might reveal nothing compared to what existed in our little boy minds. Certainly no one was killed. I doubt if anyone ever ended up in the hospital. Possibly the Carson gang exploits existed only as hearsay and legend. Whether their reputation was earned or not, we believed that it was.

One summer day when I was 7 or 8, the legend became very real. Near the corner of Grace Street and Park Avenue, there they were--at least a half dozen of them--and the race was on. Down the Grace Street hill I ran as fast as I could, and they were closing in on me fast. Across Lakeview Boulevard I sprinted and up over Petran's front and side yards, and then I hurdled the back fence paralleling Court Lane. A few more steps across the alley and I stood safely on home territory. There appeared to be an unwritten law that the gang didn't pursue a victim into his own yard. The prospect of an irate mother with a broom or garden rake kept them at bay outside that safety perimeter.

As I moved toward my basement door, I looked back and there they stood: Carson, the Teff twins, and four or five of their foot soldiers lined up along Petrans' fence yelling threats and obscenities. Whatever strength born of survival instinct and panic enabled me to sail over that fence saved me from a fate too horrible to contemplate.

Carson's ugly face and evil notoriety were now beyond debate. I would carry that image of the scene along the fence in my memory for the rest of my life. It was my bloody face, bruised body, or broken head that hung in the balance as I flew over that fence. Carson had achieved immortality. He would live forever in my memory.

Fast-forward a couple of uneventful years to the time when I was ready for my first job. I applied to the *Albert Lea Tribune* for a paper delivery route, and they informed me that I would be notified when one became available. A couple of months later the circulation manager, Russ Zavitz, called and said they had a vacancy because they were terminating the carrier for route 51. He said I should come to the *Tribune* offices after school and report to the area where the boys picked up their papers.

The place was far from posh. You had to go down through one of those iron trap doors in the sidewalk to a dingy basement room well below street level. It was like a dungeon with hard wooden benches and an opening in one wall where they handed through newspapers to each carrier as he announced his route number. The kids came, got their papers, and left one by one.

I assumed that when the kid from route 51 showed up, I was supposed to go with him to learn that route. Paper boys continued to come and go, slowed to a trickle, and then no one. Route 51 still hadn't shown up, and I was just about to go upstairs and talk to Russ when I heard footsteps descending the iron stairway. I resumed my seat, looked over toward the steps, and first saw feet, then legs, then a heavy winter jacket, and then a face and--oh my God--it was CARSON!

I quickly looked away and froze like a statue. Carson passed directly in front of me, walked up to the window and said, "Route 51." Words at this point can not express the terror that pulsed through my veins as by far the worst scourge of my young life stood before me.

Amidst the clamor in my panic stricken brain, I tried to manage at least a rational thought or two. I wondered if he noticed who I was, the kid who foiled his raid three years ago by sailing over that fence.

Carson paid no attention as he grabbed his papers, stuffed them in his canvas bag, threw the strap on his shoulder and started to leave. The thoughts in my head were so loud they must have been audible. "WHAT DO I DO NOW?" As he started up the iron staircase, I had to make a quick decision. A job hung in the balance so I had to do what Russ told me to do. I followed Carson up the steps to the sidewalk and continued to follow as he proceeded up Broadway. After half a block he obviously sensed something, stopped, turned and glared directly into my eyes.

"Are you following me?" he asked.

Trying fruitlessly to suppress my trembling jaw, I managed an anemic "yes."

"Why are you following me? Carson pressed.

"Cause I'm supposed to take your job." The tremors were not stopping.

"Whadya mean, take my job? What's going on?"

"You're being fired."

My God, I was standing there telling Carson he was being fired? Didn't he know? I stiffened as I prepared to be beaten to within an inch of my life.

"Geez--I wish somebody would tell me what's happening around this goddamn place!" he cursed as he stormed by me heading back toward the *Tribune's* front office and blasted inside. I followed but remained outside as I watched Russ and Carson through the window exchanging what appeared to be unpleasant words.

After a few tense moments, Carson left the office and confronted me out on the sidewalk. At this point, however, his mood seemed to have softened. He gave me a blank look, moved away toward the street, turned, and with a beckoning motion said, "C'mon, I'll show you the route."

Albert Lea native Paul Vinck works for Sonoma County in California, where he lives with his wife and daughter.

Recollections of Pope John Paul II
by Robert Kieffer

When Pope John Paul II was elected in 1978, I was pastor of Our Lady of Mount Carmel church in Opole. Opole is a Polish community, more so twenty-six years ago than today. The Catholic faith was strong, and I remember how proud we all were that the new Pope was Polish. The Sunday after he was elected, everyone at Sunday mass beamed.

Pope John Paul II was the topic of conversation all October. I was especially grateful for all the positive buzz because I think were all tired of those irritating Polish jokes that had been the craze.

That Christmas ABC had an idea to turn the spotlight on the faith of the Polish people in America. Someone from the chancery office in St. Cloud contacted me to see if we could manage a mass to be televised in Polish on Christmas Eve. Although I'm sure parishioners would have been able to sing the carols in Polish, no one in Opole knew less Polish than the pastor. I was grateful the parish had welcomed this Luxembourger because there were not many of us German types in Opole.

We talked it over with people in the parish and decided we would pass because it would be way too much fuss and feathers. The next October, we made up for it by taking two busloads of people to Des Moines when the Holy Father came to visit. KSTP television station in Minneapolis came to get a story before our pilgrimage to Iowa on a beautiful afternoon as we gathered in front of our church.

I had an eye opener about community roots and the sense of belonging during the interview. One of the women had answered a question asked by the newscaster, and then added, "But you should ask someone else because I'm not from here." Her statement came as a big surprise to me. The news reporter then asked her where she was from.

She responded, "I grew up in North Prairie."

"How long have you been in Opole?" asked the newscaster.

She replied, "Forty years."

None of us minded the long bus ride to Des Moines and back. It was windy and cold on that open field where the Pope celebrated mass so I made a windbreaker out of a garbage bag. We were all excited to be there. Some parishioners squirmed through the crowd to get closer to the altar, but most of us were well back in the crowd.

The helicopter arrived and landed as all of us waved, but no Holy Father got out. A second helicopter, which didn't get much of a welcome because we were wary and our enthusiasm had already been tapped, arrived with John Paul II. We thought afterwards that those two helicopters had been used as a security measure.

In 1984, when I was a pastor at St. Mary's in Breckenridge, I went on sabbatical to Rome. Included in my program of studies was an audience with Pope John Paul II. There were misguided worries about a disaffected church in the United States so the powers that be wanted to secure their ties with American priests. Therefore, American priests on sabbatical were assured of an audience with the Pope.

I was in a group of twenty-five priests invited to the Vatican. It was the noon hour, and we were going to miss lunch, and lunch at the Casa was good. Someone brought us into a large room, empty except for one large chair. Pope John Paul came in with a number of aides, sat down and delivered an exhortation. I found out that day that having an audience with the Pope means that he speaks and you listen. Afterwards he went around the room to greet us, and he gave us each a white rosary. (I gave mine to one of my nieces as a wedding gift).

When he finished greeting everyone in the group, he was standing close to me. It had been a quiet and rather somber experience, and I had an urge to reach out and touch him. As I did, his eyes looked directly into mine, and in the periphery I saw his aides move toward me.

As I was wilting, the atmosphere in the room changed. The Pope's talk became informal, he asked a few light questions, and the room was suddenly filled with priests' chatter. He gave us a blessing before he left. He was probably going to lunch, and so were we.

The official photographer was at the audience, the person who snapped pictures wherever the Pope went. That evening he brought all his pictures to the Casa and spread them out on tables. We ordered what we wanted, and I bought every picture with me in it. One of them shows only my nose.

When Pope John Paul died in 2005, a picture of us together was published in the diocesan newspaper -- he was the one in white! During his years of ministry we all grew to love him. I am now pastor of Our Lady of Victory Church in Fergus Falls. The community is predominantly Lutheran, yet it seemed everyone revered him. During the week after he died, we had prayer services for him, and we prayed that the Holy Spirit would guide the election his successor.

I talked about the Holy Father with all the students in our school and religious education classes. There were many questions, so his passing was noted. In the gathering area of the church we made a memorial display of several photos, which parishioners had acquired over the years, mine included. A young man from the parish lent us several commemorative items to add to our memorial. There was also a poster depicting all the popes from Saint Peter to John Paul II. I think there was a saint at both ends of that chart.

Father Robert Kieffer, who grew up near Morris, is pastor of Our Lady of Victory Church in Fergus Falls, where he lives with his cat Helga.

A Dog and Her Boy
by Lloyd Deuel

My dad, Ira Deuel, had foxhounds when I was young. I learned to hunt with these hounds when I was high school age. My dad was always trying to upgrade his hounds, and on June 6, 1944 (later known as D-Day), a hound that we had great hopes for had a litter of six pups. It became my job to tend to these pups. There were three males: Ranger, Cub, and Nick, and three females: Lady, Queenie, and Tripp.

The males were big and aggressive, and the females small and very shy. These dogs were of the "black and tan" breed. Before the Revolutionary War, when the sport of bull fighting with dogs was popular, this breed of dogs was used for bull fighting. They were very vicious, aggressive, and would fight and bite their handlers.

When bull fighting became unpopular, these dogs would have become extinct, except it was noted that they were exceptional at hunting game because of their keen ability to follow a game track. They were then bred to lose their viciousness, and after a few hundred dog generations of breeding, they became domesticated. When I became acquainted with these dogs, they absolutely would not bite a human under any circumstances.

I was 14 years old and knew very little about the responsibility of caring for pups, but I had lots of coaching. This was World War II time--before dog food days. I would go to the Foreston Creamery Feed Store and buy oatmeal in 25 or 50 pound bags, which I could haul on my bicycle. I would then go to the Foreston Produce, run by my Uncle Mearl and Aunt Eunice Miley, and get a pail of candled reject eggs free.

I had a 4-gallon milk pail into which I would measure a certain amount of oatmeal, add a certain amount of water, and about sixty or seventy eggs. I was told that eggshells contained protein that was good for animals. I would place this concoction on the gas stove and stir, making sure the eggs were broken, until it came to a good boil. Sometimes I would have to fine-tune this mixture with more water or oatmeal to get it just right. It had a nasty, deep yellow color, and I never tasted it, but dogs are omnivores, and the pups loved it.

After it cooled, I would dish it out into separate dishes for the pups and make sure that the bigger males did not volunteer to help the smaller females eat their share. Sometimes I would augment their meals with skim milk, which I could get free from the creamery. The pups loved milk.

These hounds had one purpose in life, and that was to follow a game track. They were in the work dog category, similar to sled dogs of the north. They were never allowed in the house, and I was the only one who bothered to pet them so we bonded.

I noticed that these pups were very much like a large human family in that they shared the same physical characteristics and quarreled with each other. However, they each had distinct personalities, which only one who knew them well could differentiate. They all excelled in hunting, as they were bred and trained to do.

In small towns at that time there were no leash laws or codes governing dogs. Dogs reproduced unrestricted, and their life span was short as they got run over by cars, trucks, and trains. To aggravate matters, there was a dog poisoner who would bait poison for dogs. Dad built a fenced-in kennel to keep his dogs safe and at home, which helped somewhat, but he avoided tying these dogs on a chain.

Minnesota State Highway 23 ran through Foreston between St Cloud and Milaca, and it was a busy road. One day Tripp saw me on the other side of the road and came bounding across to greet me. A big semi-truck and trailer was traveling too fast to slow down or stop, and Tripp was caught between the front wheels. She tumbled the full length of the truck and trailer on the underneath side, but avoided the wheels and emerged at the rear. I carried her home, and my dad and I examined her the best we could. We could find no broken bones or wounds, but she was very sore and stiff for awhile.

It was as though she had been given a lecture like one would give a child, "Do not walk on the road, and look both ways before crossing." This dog remembered that episode for the rest of her life. Unfortunately, her five litter mates all fell victims to truck or car or train before they reached their fourth year.

Tripp became my dad's best hunting dog. She was never disciplined, as she never did anything to warrant scolding. She was so shy that when people came to visit, they never knew this dog lived at our home, as she would disappear when a car drove into the yard. I was the only person who had petted her for the first ten years of her life.

When my son Scott was two years old, his mother and I would take him to visit his Grandpa and Grandma Deuel on their farm on the edge of Foreston. It was a cold, blustery spring morning, and Scott wanted to play outside on his tricycle by the back steps. It was too cold to be outside with him, and it was warmer to watch him through the window. A farmer came down the muddy road driving a noisy tractor pulling a farm wagon. Scott abandoned the tricycle and started for the road. From nowhere Tripp came and stood crossways between Scott and the road so that he could not get around her. He did get to pet her for the first time.

When Tripp repeated this act four more times that morning, we realized that Scott had baby sitter, friend, and companion. We visited my parents nearly every weekend, and sometimes Scott would stay with them for a week at a time. He dearly loved exploring that farm, and Tripp was his constant companion-- except when he went into the house, and then she stayed outside.

My dad had cows on his small farm, but not enough pasture so he rented land across the road. He built a fence lane going north, then west, and back south to the road. Twice a day he would have to drive his cows around this lane because they would dally if he didn't. He would watch for traffic on the road, open the gate, drive them across and then close the gate on the other side.

When Scott came to visit, he taught him to drive the cows around the lane, and Scott and Tripp did this happily and proudly. When my dad was questioned about the safety of a 4-year-old driving cows, he pointed out that Tripp was always between the boy and cows. There would be no cow hurting her boy. My dad went on to state that he always wanted a good cattle dog and now he thought he had one with Tripp. When Scott went home, however, he found that Tripp lost all interest in cows.

That summer my dad had his hay baled. It was a fine crop, and he underestimated the number of bales he would have. The crew guessed how big the baled haystack would be and started on this huge stack. When they reached the point where they should have stopped, they had many more bales to stack, and their solution was to just build it higher. When the stack was finished, and it was time for the stackers on top to come down, my dad's extension ladder was too short. He had to park his hay rack next to the stack and place the ladder on top. The ladder barely reached, but if one was careful, it was judged to be safe.

One day when Scott was visiting the farm, my dad was working away from home. My mother found Scott and Tripp playing on top of the haystack, and immediately called my dad to come home to get him down. When my dad came home, he realized that he had moved the ladder off the wagon, but still left it leaning on the stack. The ladder was in the upright position and nearly straight up and down. The top rung of the ladder was about a foot and a half from reaching the top of the haystack, which made for an extremely dangerous and nearly impossible position to use. My dad started his tractor, hooked on his hay rack, and drove it next to the stack. He moved the ladder back up onto the hay rack, put a long rope on his shoulder, and climbed to the top of haystack. He made a sling around Scott and lowered him down to my mother. Dad did the same for Tripp. As soon as he got down, he lowered the ladder and put it in its proper rack. All this time he listened to instructions from my mother as to how he should have done this in the first place.

When Scott was asked how he had gotten on top of the haystack and how he managed to get Tripp up there, he could not remember. Some of our friends asked, "How did that dog ever get that kid up there?"

When our daughter Jean was a year and a half old, she was fascinated by my dad's dogs. He had acquired four more, and old Tripp was the leader that could be depended upon to train them properly. Jean would stand outside the kennel gate and try to pet them. She could not quite reach through the netting, so she pulled the pin on the gate latch. The gate flew open, and dogs spilled out. The first dog tried to stop, but the others pushed him over Jean, knocking her down. The rest tried to avoid her by jumping over her as she rolled over in the grass screaming.

She was bundled up and not hurt or scratched. However it was noted that she had an extremely loud, far reaching voice similar to my dad's. A half a cookie later she was all healed, but the terrified dogs disappeared.

The dogs did not come home that day. The next morning my dad reported they had been home during the night to eat their food, but had left again. Scott and Jean ventured out in the yard after breakfast, and were all set for a day of exploring the farm. A noisy truck came down the road, and Jean started toward it. Tripp appeared out of nowhere and stood between her and the road. Jean was able to pet Tripp.

Thinking back on this remarkable dog, one has to note that she spent the first two-thirds of her life as an almost invisible dog that had no people interaction. She did not respond to calling except when she was hunting. She had no training except for hunting. Little kids had never played with her until Scott and Jean came along.

All of the protective traits she showed toward them were instinctive. She had learned her lesson about crossing roads, and it had stayed with her. Most of her sibling litter mates had lucked out on their first encounter with cars and trucks, but had succumbed on the next encounter. Tripp had used her experience and applied it with Scott and Jean for great results. She fully enjoyed the interaction with kids that she missed when she was younger. Tripp proved to be a remarkable dog and companion.

Lloyd Deuel, a five-time Minnesota Memories contributor, is a retired machinist living in Brooklyn Center. He and his wife Phyllis enjoy gardening and woodworking.

Starter Car
by Steve Swanson

In the spring of 1948, my next-door neighbor, Dickie Jacobson, and I formed a corporation and bought our first car. We each paid $12.50. Our $25 bought a 1926 Model T Ford Touring Car that had sat behind Friggie's Bar unused for several years. It had no top, and the seats were rotted away. The tires were flat, but it was beautiful.

We pumped up the tires, towed it home and got it running. Underneath the back seat we found war souvenirs--a rusted Samurai sword, a trench shovel, a stained Japanese flag and a pair of moldy combat boots.

Someone had customized Henry Ford's standard black by painting our car's body Kelly green. Its fenders were canary yellow and the wooden spokes were alternately yellow and green. The Northfield police always knew exactly where in town our green and yellow Model T was. There was no other car even remotely like it in seven counties. We got by with nothing at all.

Dick and I shared for a couple of months, but soon we both seemed to want the car at the same time for private sorties. I finally bought him out, and for an additional $12.50 the car was mine.

Today's drivers would be threatened by the utter simplicity of the Model T Ford: no gas gauges or idiot lights, no radio, no heater. What good would it do with no top and no windows? The dashboard had only an ignition switch and a light switch. You checked the fuel supply by standing up, leaning over the windshield, unscrewing the gas cap and looking into the tank.

Driving the three-pedal Model T was simple. You pushed one pedal down to start out from a stop, released it to go faster (35 miles per hour maximum). If you held the forward pedal halfway and pressed the reverse pedal, you'd go backwards. For a panic stop you could press all three pedals at the same time.

No transmission system ever worked better for rocking out of mud or snow. You could get into a smooth rhythmic forward and reverse motion by moving those pedals up and down and by controlling the speed with the hand throttle on the steering column.

Every kid in town rode in my car. No one ever opened the doors because they just jumped on the running board, vaulted over the door and squeezed in. I kept the car for a couple of years, then opted for a sedan that was faster, better-equipped, dryer in rain, warmer in snow, less conspicuous and more romantic.

Joey Roderick was younger and needed a starter car so I sold him my car for $75, thus tripling my original investment. Joey was not taken to the cleaners on the deal, however. He drove my Model T for awhile, then parked it in a shed. Thirty years later he resurrected it and towed it to his home in Denver. Last time I heard, it was worth $5000.

A touring car in its prime

Rubber Gun Wars
by Steve Swanson

In 1943, we sixth graders, when the school year finally ended, planned rubber-gun wars. Today's parents would be appalled: "A war? With guns?" I don't claim it was right, only fun.

The latex rubber inner tube was used for nearly a half century, from the time the pneumatic auto tire was invented to the time Japanese forces took control of rubber plantations in the Indies and forced chemists to invent vinyl.

Latex inner tubes were flowerpot red and very snappy and stretchy. Damaged ones could be had for free from most gas stations. With a sharp scissors, which sometimes caused blisters on your fingers, you cut the tube transversely into one-half inch rings. Unlike converging longitude in northern Canada, where correction lines turned every tenth section of land into a trapezoid to get a north-pointing boundary again, inner tube rings diverged. About every third ring was three quarters of an inch wider at the outside and had to be re-cut. A tight knot in the middle of each ring made a flying figure eight and minimized wind resistance.

The rubber gun itself was cut from orange crate lumber and had a clamp in back, usually a snap clothespin. One end of the six-inch rubber strap was pinched into that. You stretched the end over the fourteen-inch gun barrel.

When you pushed the clothespin open with the heel of your hand, the band would snap forward with a range of about thirty feet. Up close, a direct hit would hurt.

We also made machine guns that had about six notches toward the back. A cloth strap could be molded down into the notches. With a rubber band in each notch, you could fire from one to six bands instantly just by lifting the strap.

Like our far more vulnerable fathers and brothers, who were back then immersed in fighting World War II, we acknowledged generals, chose up armies, and declared war.

Unless you were Superman, speed and agility wouldn't work in a real war, but for rubber gun battles, as in dodge ball, they were great assets because when you were hit, you were out. The last survivor's side won.

There were penalties about lying about a hit, aiming for someone's face, or for cowardice in the face of short-range shots. The rarest form of battlefield justice was the firing squad. It happened to me once. I was stood up against a tree, my bare back exposed, then some sadistic youth discharged a machine gun point blank. Not being able to see the ensuing six red welts helped repress my tears.

It's probably good that there are no more red latex inner tubes, although the BB gun wars that we graduated to in junior high were far more risky and painful.

Rubber gun battles sometimes spilled over from fun to brutal, and obviously they were fought with confrontational indoctrination. But like less bellicose games, they also included teamwork, honesty, ingenuity, courage, stoicism, fairness and camaraderie. Today's parents would never allow it, but back then we all somehow survived.

Northfield resident Steve Swanson is an author of mystery books for young readers, a retired St. Olaf English professor, and a member of the Lutheran clergy.

Limousine
by Ross Plovnick

Some deeds we need to do right now, before the moment slips away. This is a lesson I learned from experience.

My mother-in-law, Ida Bruder Yasgur, was born in 1915 in Minsk, Belarus, where she spent most of her life. A steadfast Communist, she managed a bakery for many years. She gave birth to three children, but in the war-ravaged Soviet Union, two of them died in the early 1940s, one of pneumonia and the other of starvation. Soon after the Nazis invaded in 1941, Ida fled with her husband and a few relatives to Sverdlovsk in Siberia. When the war ended, they returned to Minsk, where she gave birth to her daughter Liza in 1947.

By 1989, when I married Liza in Minneapolis, Ida was a widow who had lived in Minnesota for eight years. Although she spoke and understood little English and never drove a car, she maintained her independence, living alone in an apartment in St. Louis Park two blocks from where we lived. She delighted in cooking meals and baking fancy pastries for our family and in making savory beet and spinach soups. Plants filled her small apartment, and on her tiny balcony she grew tomatoes in pots each summer. Ida loved to make things grow, and she loved fresh fruits and vegetables.

For years, most Saturday mornings from late May through mid-October, I had a date with Ida. I picked her up before 8 a.m. and drove her to the outdoor Farmers' Market in Minneapolis, where she would buy a week's supply of fruits, vegetables, and often fresh-cut flowers. She brought along her own bags and insisted on carrying her share of the load. Gradually I learned enough Russian to communicate with her, including the words for all the foods she bought at the market.

The Farmers' Market was enchanting with crisp, early morning temperatures, and sunlight streaming in to set moist produce aglow. Aromas of freshly brewed coffee, just-baked breads, spicy apple cider, chives, onions, and flowers filled the space.

Vendors and customers bargained in exotic languages and dialects. A kaleidoscopic crowd of diverse sizes and ages and appearances overflowed the narrow aisles. Lilting music of guitar, violin and clarinet prompted passersby to drop coins or bills into gaping instrument cases.

Ida was quiet while we drove to the market, but she came alive like a child when we arrived. She carefully inspected each fruit or vegetable before getting down to the serious business of negotiating price. Her negotiations were fascinating; she bartered with vendors who spoke Vietnamese, Cambodian, Laotian, Hmong, and Spanish, cutting her deals with a combination of hand gestures, pointing fingers, and a smattering of broken English. I watched, helped carry bags, and drove.

On the way home we sometimes stopped at Ida's favorite fish market, which added to the odor in my car trunk at the end of our expeditions. An astute shopper, she always shared her purchases generously with our family.

Occasionally we brought along Ida's Russian neighbors, Jenya and Arkady. I marveled at their determination and vitality. They all lived in their own apartments and asserted their independence by shopping for themselves. Although they were elderly and not in the best of health, they were tough survivors. Whenever I was away and could not drive them to the market, they went by bus. I don't know how they managed with their heavy bags.

Which brings me to the deed I needed to do before the moment slipped away. Ida was more than 80 years old, slowed, and bent with ailments that included arthritis, heart disease and diabetes, but she still asked to shop at the Farmers' Market.

I thought that as a special tribute I would hire a limousine to pick her up with her neighbors one Saturday and drive them in style to the Farmers' Market and home again. I thought she would treasure the experience, and I imagined a limousine filled with produce and happy friends. I thought of hiring that limousine, but I didn't do it.

A month before her eighty-second birthday, Ida's health failed to the point that she had to give up her apartment and move into a nursing home. As she became weaker and weaker, we saw the sparkle leave her eyes and watched her strong spirit, which had sustained her through a difficult life, deteriorate. Four months later she died.

Now Liza and I visit Ida's gave. We place flowers she would love at the headstone and remember her with love. And I remember our visits to the Farmers' Market and think about the limousine ride I wish I had given her.

Ida, granddaughter Jackie, and daughter Liza

Ross Plovnick, born in North Carolina and raised in Massachusetts, has lived and worked in Minnesota for 34 years. A retired chemist, he and his wife Liza enjoy world travel.

Testing Survival Of The Fittest
by Menno "Spike" Dammer

Growing up on a farm in southwestern Minnesota is often a challenge because the weather can change in a matter of minutes, and immediate adjustments must be made with livestock, crops, and anything else when you need to batten down the hatches. Sometimes we are responsible for creating emergency situations on our own, however, and such was the case in my fifth year, 1935, when life was as real as it gets.

Although we had a tractor to provide power for the majority of our farm work, it was still a time when many jobs were performed with horses, and what follows is as clear an experience for me as if it had happened only yesterday. How I survived, one may wonder, but you will see why I chose the title I did for this memory.

One of Dad's favorite working teams was Heine and Frankie because they were strong and young and could stand the heat and humidity better than most of our other horses. On this particular day, my dad brought the team in from using them in harness and took them to the farmyard water tank for a drink before they went into the barn. The horses were so well trained that they walked to the tank on their own, and when they were satisfied, they took the walk to the barn, still in harness, which was about one hundred feet away.

My memory kicks in here because I was sitting on the stoop of the open barn door through which Heine and Frankie had to enter to get to their respective stalls. I don't recall what I was doing, but the next thing I saw when I looked up was Heine, spooked, and proceeding to jump over me, into the barn. One of his hoofs hit me flat and square in the forehead and so I took a tumble, head over teakettle, into the barn.

Heine continued on through the barn without stopping at his stall and dashed out the open back door into the pasture. While my dad heard this commotion and tried to come to my aid, my mom was even closer outside. When she heard me cry, she thought it would be the last sound I might ever make because no little 5- year-old kid could ever survive being kicked in the head by a horse--but I did.

Aside from being scared and having a dirty face, my injury was slight because I must have rolled with the blow. Washing my face and putting on a little ointment, which in those days was usually Vicks Vapo-Rub as a cure-all, was all my mom had to do. Little did I realize there was more to come.

When my barn experience with Heine had been all but forgotten, and it was about a week later, according to my mom's recollection, I was bringing my dad his afternoon lunch in a field about a mile away. Again, he had Heine and Frankie as a team on the mower he was using. When you are a 5- year-old with a curious nature about everything in life, you don't just sit with your dad while he eats his lunch. You climb onto the round metal seat of the mower, where you are bound to make some kind of noise that could spook most animals, especially a horse like Heine. Before Dad could get up and pull me from my perch on that mower, Heine and Frankie took off like heigh-ho-Silver, and they were on their way down that gravel road that lead to home. Farm horses would always run for the farmyard, no matter what the circumstances were, so I knew where we were headed, but all I could do was secure a firm grip on that seat beneath me and hang on.

It was one bumpy ride, and along the way parts from that mower were coming loose and whizzing by my head. I can still see and feel that ride down that road and over the hill past the gravel pit and into the driveway to our farmyard. When the horses came to a stop, the mower didn't look like a mower anymore, and it took my mom's gentle touch after she rushed outside hearing all the noise, to pry my hands from the grip I still had on that seat. I was pretty shook up but no worse for wear. It just seemed to be part of a day's work on the farm.

These are two of my not-so-favorite experiences on the farm, and yet they are two things I never will forget. My dad sold Heine a short time after these incidents. We had a few laughs over those incidents many years later, but it sure wasn't funny at the time. I know my mom earned more than a few gray hairs that week, and I sometimes wonder if my parents would have been better off keeping Heine and getting rid of me instead. Ah memories...

Ellsworth native Menno Dammer, retired from the Los Angeles County Sheriff Department, writes a weekly editorial that can be read at http://www.lasdretired.org

Exploring *America*
by Don Matejcek

The steamer *America* launched its maiden voyage on Saturday, April 2, 1898, less than a month after its manufacturing was completed at the Detroit Dry Dock. It was intended for daily service on Lake Michigan between Michigan City and Chicago, and Chicago marine men, who expressed their satisfaction with the ship, remarked about its speed of 15 to 18 miles per hour.

Booth Steamship Line purchased the steamer in 1902 and put *America* on its Duluth, Port Arthur and Isle Royal route. In 1911 the ship underwent extensive expansion in West Superior, Wisconsin. The renovation project extended its hull 18 feet beyond its original 154 feet. This additional space made room for twelve staterooms that could accommodate as many as fifty additional passengers and freight capacity to accommodate one hundred additional tons.

Many years later, *America's* 1928 season began normally, and there were no signs that this would be its final year. On Wednesday, June 6, 1928, *America* steamed out of the Duluth Ship Canal and headed up the north shore, where plans included stopping at all the ports of call. From Grand Marais it headed toward Isle Royale, Michigan, to drop off a number of passengers.

Soon after clearing the dock at Isle Royale's Washington Harbor, Captain Smith turned command over to First Mate John Wick with Fred Nelson at the wheel. Five minutes later *America* thudded over a reef, bumping four times and tearing a small hole through its bottom below the engine room on the starboard side.

At first it seemed as though *America's* pumps could handle the water rushing in, but chief engineer Frank McMillan quickly reassessed the situation and determined that *America* was going to sink. Captain Smith returned to the bridge to find Wick ringing the bell to alert all aboard of the disaster. Moments later Smith yelled, "Beach her! Beach her!"

Captain Smith remembered a small gravel beach in the north gap of Washington Harbor, a good place to try to nose *America* ashore before she foundered in deep water. He ordered Fred Nelson to swing the wheel and point *America* directly toward that beach. They heard another thud, and *America* stopped 300 yards short of the beach that would have assured imminent salvage, subsequent repair and return to service. Unfortunately, the stern was hanging out over 85 feet of water, so as it sank, it slid off into deep water.

America was tied more to the people of Isle Royale than any of the other ships that remained in its waters, and it was also tied to those who lived along the Lake Superior shore between Duluth and Thunder Bay. Few vessels are recalled with more genuine affection than the popular *America,* and the popularity was renewed with the advent of scuba diving. *America* is by far the most dived shipwreck at Isle Royal National Park, which is 20 miles from Minnesota and 85 miles from Michigan. I know it belongs to Michigan, but I've always considered it Minnesota's.

In the late 1960s, members of my Owatonna Scuba Diving Club began diving on the *America,* and in the late '70s, I started taking 8 mm movies of it. A diver friend of mine from Faribault was speaking to a ladies' group about our dive and showing my movies when a woman from the back of the room spoke up and said she knew someone who was on the *America* when it sank.

She gave my friend the names of Leland and Lyman Clay, twin brothers from St. Charles who were rescued that day. Every summer their dad, Dr. F. H. Clay, had sent them up to their vacation cabin on Isle Royale to relieve their allergies. It turns out that this is really a small world. We found out that Dr. Clay had delivered Drs. John and Ken Henry, who were then my doctors in Owatonna.

There was a Dr. Clay living at Lutsen, so I called him up. He turned out to be one of the twins who had been on the *America* that day. His brother, who was also a doctor, was visiting him from California so we set up a time when we could drive up to Lutsen to talk to them about the sinking.

Dr. Clay told me that when we arrived in Lutsen we would see an Electric Co-op sign on the left and on the right we would see a power pole with “Clay” lettered on it, and that was their driveway.

My wife and I and our two sons and a friend and his wife all had a long talk with the two brothers. They were teens when the ship sank, and their dad always figured they were joking around, trying to play pranks on people. When they got back to the mainland and called their dad, he didn’t believe at first that the *America* had actually sunk.

The only life lost on the *America* was the Clay brothers’ dog, which was tied to the stern flagpole. There was a new 1928 Model T pickup in the cargo hole, and it is still there. The remains of a piano are still on the promenade deck, and there are many artifacts still on the ship. That’s one reason why the wreck is so much fun to dive.

When the Clay brothers got into their lifeboat, they still had their room key, and when we talked to them, they showed it to us--hanging on the wall in Lutsen.

The *Kamloops* was a shipwreck that everyone tried to find from the time it sank in 1927 until the time they found it in 1977. The Clays told us that if anyone had asked, they could have taken divers right out to the site. A few days after the *Kamloops* sank, the boys paddled their canoe and tried to pull rolls of wire that had floated to the surface from the ship. The twins had heard that the *Kamloops* was carrying Canadian whiskey, and the boys were sure they could pull some up with that wire. They nearly tipped their canoe, but didn’t get any whiskey.

When we were driving up to Isle Royale the last few years, I noticed that there wasn’t any Clay name on the power pole so I decided to stop and see if I could find out what had happened to the Clays.

After talking to the new owners of the property, I was able to locate the doctor’s son, John Clay, who lives in Montana. I learned that his folks had died, but that his uncle, now in this 90s, was doing fine in California. In fact, he was still going to the gym every day in 2004.

I've been a member of the Owatonna Scuba Diving Club for over forty years, and I've gone on a lot of dives in various places that have given me some good stories to tell. But this is one of my best stories. After diving the *America* for so many years, I felt privileged and lucky to interview two of the survivors of that famous 1928 wreck. What a great experience it was to speak with the Clay brothers.

America

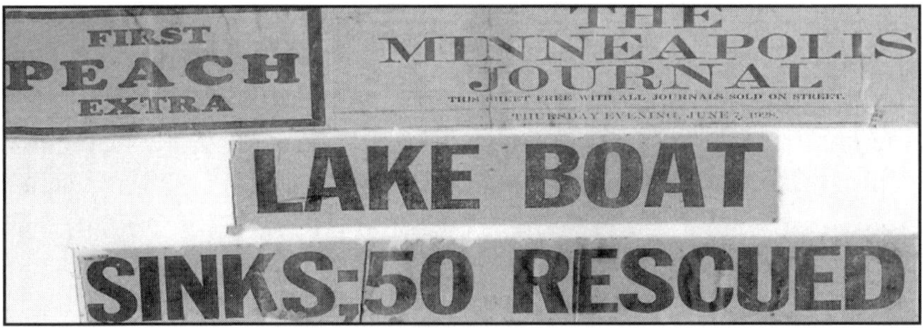

FIRST PEACH EXTRA

THE MINNEAPOLIS JOURNAL

LAKE BOAT SINKS; 50 RESCUED

News headlines from 1928

Clay Boys Escape as Steamer Sinks

Five-time contributor Don Matejcek grew up and worked in Owatonna. Now retired from Owatonna Public Utilities, Don enjoys diving.

The Shopping Trip
by Betsy Hermanson

When the weather turned cold near the end of 1958 and the Mankato hills and valleys were covered with the first winter snows, Janet, Mimo and I began planning a Christmas shopping trip.

We saved our allowances and did extra chores and carefully counted our dimes, nickels and pennies. Finally we had enough money to buy gifts for our families, and then enough extra change to finish our shopping excursion with a refreshing cup of hot chocolate at one of the downtown lunch counters.

On the next Saturday morning, we set out. I walked over to Janet's house on Dickenson Street, right behind Washington School and just down the street from those strange half-circled metal silos laid sideways on the ground, known as "the Quonsets," apartments which housed the post-war influx of married college students. Together Janet and I walked down East Main and picked up Mimo before heading down the hill.

Mankato's Main Street hill is a wonderful road; it curves ever so gently over its crest, then plunges rider or walker headlong down six city blocks to the river valley below. It is steep – in fact, one of my high school teachers once confessed that as a high schooler himself, he and some friends had waited until two or three in the morning when there was little chance of traffic, then set their sled in the middle of the street at the very top and tobogganed down the hill. As he told it, the daredevil group ended up across the railroad tracks, across the bridge, and somewhere along the main street of North Mankato. He always ended this story by warning us never to be foolish enough to try it ourselves.

Tobogganing the hill wasn't in our plan for the day. Our trio of giggling girls walked down the snow-covered sidewalks past the tipsy-looking houses that balanced sideways on precarious slopes, past the Andrew Carnegie library on the left, and KYSM radio station on the right, and down to Salet's Department Store at the corner of Front and Main.

Where should we begin? Mimo came from a large family, so she had the most to buy for. Janet had only two sisters, while I had three sisters and a brother. We probably cruised through Salet's, which was a moderately priced department store. Perhaps we even walked the magical aisles of Brett's, a higher-priced department store that was beyond our simple means. To get the most for our money, we headed for the central block of downtown Mankato which had three dime stores in a row: Woolworth's, Kresge's and H.L. Green.

In 1958, dime stores still carried many things that cost only a dime, or at least well under a dollar. And when young girls had only a couple of dollars to spread among family members, every penny counted. I don't remember what items we actually purchased, but I know the types of things we might have chosen. There were chiffon scarves or pretty hankies for our older sisters and Little Golden books for the younger ones.

Or maybe we got paper dolls, those wonderful booklets that cost about 29 cents. They had cardboard dolls on the front and back covers, already perforated so they could just be punched out and ready to dress. The inside pages were filled with wonderful costumes for the beach, the bedroom or the fancy dress ball. We all played with paper dolls – begged our mothers for small boxes, spare shoeboxes or handkerchief boxes which we filled with doll families, bridal parties or even the lovely Lennon sisters from TV's *Lawrence Welk Show*. Of course, we were 12 and 13 - getting too old for dolls – but we might play with these while keeping watch over our younger siblings.

Not surprisingly, the main gift each of us was looking for that day was the gift for our mother. Our moms were special--not the perfectly-coiffed June Cleaver, who dusted and vacuumed across the black and white picture tube in our living room wearing high heels, pearls and earrings. Our moms were more practical, wearing everyday house dresses with hair that got mussed and tempers that occasionally frayed. But they were always there for us with Kool-Aid and cookies for snacks, an extra place at the supper table for a friend, or an extra pillow if someone decided to sleep over.

Now as we wandered the creaky wooden floors of the store aisles, the three of us spotted the perfect present for our wonderful mothers. There in front of us on a counter was a whole display of tiny glass perfume bottles. They were shaped like miniature kerosene lanterns, and each had a shiny plastic shade of a different color--red, blue, amber or green. They cost 39 cents.

After fingering each bottle and counting the cost, after agonizing over the color (I chose blue, because my mom had a beautiful, blue-quilted boxed set of Evening in Paris perfume, and I thought this would match perfectly) we made our way to the nearest cash register and, carefully counting out the coins from our purses, made our purchases.

Balancing those paper sacks along with our other gifts, we rushed out the doors and were caught up in the busy sidewalk traffic of holiday shoppers. Suddenly, with a push or shove from an unknown passerby, Mimo gasped as a package slipped from her grip, and with a clink and a tinkle, the strong scent of perfume rose from the sidewalk to hit our noses and then our brains as we realized a tragedy had just occurred.

Mimo began to cry. Janet and I circled our friend to protect her from other shoppers as we tried to comfort her until the sobs subsided. Then we held a cabinet level meeting right there on the sidewalk, and the traffic had to weave around us as we decided what to do next.

"We can just go back in and buy another bottle," we stated, smug in our assurance that the problem was solved.

"But I don't have enough money!" Mimo wailed as she began to cry once more.

The awfulness of this problem registered on each of our faces in turn, and without speaking, Janet and I knew. We all pulled out our plastic wallets from inside our plastic purses and began to count our remaining change. Yes, we all had at least a dime, because we were planning to have hot cocoa at one of the dime stores. Were there enough pennies? Yes, between the three of us, there were! We had 39 cents!

There was no cocoa purchased that day; there was no swinging of feet and twirling of stools beside the high lunch counter; there was no sipping sweet chocolate and bobbing of giant marshmallows with our spoons. But we were comfortably warmed as we turned the corner from Front to Main Street, felt the sting of cold wind across our cheeks and started the long trudge back up the big hill. Mimo was secure in the knowledge of good friends and the fact that she did have a present for her mother after all. And Janet and I were filled with a new and pleasant feeling that made us feel very adult. By giving up some small thing for ourselves, we had made another person happy. Surprisingly, that felt a lot better than a whole pot of hot cocoa.

Downtown Mankato in the '50s.
Photo courtesy of Blue Earth County Historical Sociey

Betsy Hermanson and her husband Ross have lived in Wells for 30 years. They have five adult children and they enjoy being grandparents.

A Long Life in Freeborn County
by Leona Scherb

After my parents died of tuberculosis when I was 8 years old in 1924, I went to live with my grandparents on a farm between Emmons and Albert Lea.

Times were tough then. I went to Gilbert Rolvang School until sixth grade. The boys at school would go to the neighbor's house to get water every day. One bucket lasted all day; everyone drank from the same dipper. There was no kindergarten, just first through eighth grade. When my brother started school, he could not speak English, only Norwegian. He wasn't the only one; many could only speak Norwegian or German. At our home we talked only Norwegian, and ate lots of lefse and lutefisk. I wish I could remember how to speak Norwegian now.

Our country school was heated by a wood or coal-burning stove. The floors were always cold, as we didn't have basements, and we always had cold feet. Because our feet were cold all the time, we would get chilblains, blue swollen infections on the soles of the feet. One boy had them so much he would swing his feet all day long to pump up his blood circulation, and it seemed to help. We had outdoor toilets, and they were cold. On Halloween night the boys would tip over outhouses. First thing in the morning after Halloween we would look out hoping our outhouse wasn't tipped over. Those were the good old days!

We used buggies and sleighs because there were very few cars. They cost about $400, so few people could afford them. They had to be started by cranking, and that could be difficult. Sometimes there was a kick back; you could break your arm trying to start the car. There were no snowplows so when snow banks were large, sometimes the sleigh would tip over on its side, and everyone would get out and tip it up again.

During the Depression, money was scarce. Our sandwiches for school were homemade bread with onions and maybe a dill pickle made from a cucumber from our garden. My uncle and aunt had nine children. Every day she would make eight loaves of bread. The children would come to the table hungry, and rather than take time to slice the bread, she would tear it apart and give each one a big hunk of it. Another meal was homemade bread with sour cream over it and a third layer of sauce.

I can remember the julebukkers coming to our house between Christmas and New Years. This was a Norwegian custom, and they would go from farm to farm. If there was room for the horses, they went into the barn; otherwise they would wait outside. The horses were trained to wait and never ran away. The julebukkers were dressed in terrible old clothes, and would not knock, but would come right in. They were neighbors dressed so no one would know them, and we were to guess who they were and invite them in for Christmas goodies and coffee. A friend of mine was so afraid that when they came to her house, she would hide under the bed until they left. I dressed up as a tramp and went julebukking too.

We had no electricity in those days so we would take an evergreen tree from a neighbor's yard for Christmas and put lighted candles on it. Houses were heated with wood-burning stoves on the first floor. If we didn't have an icebox to keep food cold, we would put it in the basement because there was no heat down there.

For fun we would slide down the hill in a dishpan, running water on the hill to make it slippery. We went to church by sleigh in the winter and buggy in the summer. In the winter when we rode in the sleigh, we would cover up with a horsehair blanket and heat stones or bricks in the fire, then put them in the sleigh to keep us warm.

I don't think I came to Albert Lea until we had a car. When we did get to Albert Lea, seeing that big, high building, the Hyde Building, was great, and going to the 10-cents store and eating at the lunch counter was another treat. We called it the 10-cents store, not Woolworth's.

When I was about 12 or 13, I taught myself how to drive a car in our pasture. We lived on a farm. I hit the gate coming around the corner, and my grandfather told me to wait a couple years before driving again. We could drive at any age and didn't need a license. Then the time came when everyone had to buy a license, but we didn't have to take a test. The driver's license cost 35 cents.

I met my husband at a dance in Lake Mills when I was 17. We didn't want anyone to sign for our marriage license, so we waited to marry until we were 18 and 21. We lived in Kiester after we were married, and then moved to Albert Lea. I have lived in my current house 65 years; I don't believe in moving very often.

We were married in 1933, and I worked at the telephone office in Kiester, where my pay was $5 a week. There was a large screen to sit by, and someone would call in and give me the name of the person they wanted to talk to, and I would ring them up. Households all had different rings like two short rings, one long and two short, or three long, etc. I either knew these rings, or I could look them up in a book. Everyone with a phone would hear these rings, and they could go to the telephone on their wall and listen in on other peoples' conversations. This should not have happened, but it did happen all day long; people would hear the gossip that way. There was no TV or radio, so people would listen in on the telephone--if they had one. Not everyone did. Whenever there was a fire, I would get the call and have to go out and blow the whistle so the whole town would hear it. Someone would have to be in the telephone building day and night to receive urgent calls. If someone passed away, the church bell would ring one time for each year old the person was.

When we moved to Albert Lea in 1940, there were only three other houses in our neighborhood, and there were cows in the pasture across the street where Grace Lutheran Church is now. I am a charter member of Grace Lutheran Church, a spin-off of First Lutheran, which had more than 5000 members. At first we met at Northside Bank, then moved the church to a Quonset hut before the current church was built in the 1950s. I taught Sunday school for years, and my husband was one of the head ushers.

In the Quonset church we had eight weddings a year; in the 1980s there were twenty-eight per year. For thirty-six years I was wedding coordinator. I was directress of the Altar Guild two times. A friend and I would bring communion to the homebound for many years. I resigned at 86 years of age. Now others in the church bring communion to me.

I loved to sew and made most of my clothes, my daughter's clothes and our coats through the years. I sewed curtains for the church. Ladies Aid had a mother/daughter lunch, but we had no money for table decorations. I made new clothes for some of my daughter's dolls, and they were our table decorations. Everyone liked them.

My daughter Jeane received a pin for perfect attendance at Sunday school for 13 years. She says when it was hot, she went to Sunday school; when it was cold, she went to Sunday school; when she was sick, she went to Sunday school. I said she would always get sick in the middle of the week, and by Sunday she was well. I also earned a pin for perfect attendance teaching Sunday school for seven years. Then I got sick and that broke my record; I had to start counting all over again.

I love flowers and have lots of flowers growing around my house in the summer. If they needed flowers for church services, I would enjoy bringing them over. I also brought pussy willows in the spring. If my flowers were in pots, they were heavy. I would put them in my red wagon, pull it across the street, up the ramp and into the church and unload them in front of the altar.

I traveled to Branson seven times. My favorite show there and on television is *Lawrence Welk*. My friends know not to call me on Saturday evening because I watch his video three times. I also went to Europe twice. Switzerland was my favorite country; I especially liked all the flowers in window boxes.

I have been blessed with a long life and good health, until I got arthritis a few years ago. I miss doing things I used to do, but the time has come when I am unable to get around very much. I watch Sunday church services on TV. My daughter helps me a lot, and I have her dog, which keeps me company. I feel like I took care of myself, and I'm enjoying this time of my life. Even though I've always lived within twenty miles of where I was born, I've seen a lot of change, done many things, gone a lot of places, cultivated many interests and lived a good life for over ninety years.

Little Leona and others on the porch of her home in the 1920s

Taking Grandpa Lunch
by MicheLe L. Larson

Rural life has different patterns and rhythms than the urban experience. Certainly the pace is different. The population is usually different. The choices, whether it's shopping or entertainment, are different. Sometimes even the names of the meals are different.

While I was growing up in southwestern Minnesota, we spent lots of time on Grandpa and Grandma's farm, especially during summer. There were always five meals on the farm: a big country breakfast, morning lunch, dinner (which is what the noon meal was called), afternoon lunch, and supper. Lunch, especially afternoon lunch, was a favorite time because by then, the better part of another day was finished. Afternoon lunch meant there were only another few hours of work before a little evening relaxation, and finally, a good night's sleep.

When the children visited the farm, especially in the summer, they looked forward to afternoon lunch. Sometimes Grandpa and Uncle Thomas would take their lunch into the fields with them, or they might come back to the house for lunch, but other times, Grandma and the children would take lunch out to them in the field.

Grandma's lunches usually consisted of bread, butter, and sandwiches, made with her homemade strawberry jam. There were also homemade donuts, or some of her sugar cookies, or maybe as a special treat, some of her homemade cinnamon rolls. If Grandpa and Uncle Thomas weren't coming back to the house, Grandma, Mom, and the children would eat lunch together. Grandma always made her special Kool-Aid for the grandchildren. It was usually orange or green Kool-Aid, but she mixed in a can of orange juice concentrate for more flavor.

When they were finished with lunch, Grandma made fresh coffee and put it in a thermos. She then packed sandwiches, donuts and cookies into the old black metal lunch pail to take to Grandpa and Uncle Thomas. Sometimes she had an extra thermos of the Kool-Aid that she packed too. If the children were within earshot, she would ask if they wanted to come with her. Since it sounded like such a great adventure, the children always said yes.

Grandma went out to the step with the lunch pail and found her walking stick. Then she and the children set off on their journey, with Grandma's little brown dog Mitzi trotting beside them.

They walked past the machine shed, through the woods, past the big, new, steel machine shed, to the edge of the field. They could hear tractors in the distance, so they knew they wouldn't have to wait very long. On those hot summer afternoons, they enjoyed standing under trees, listening to birds and crickets as the wind rustled the leaves of the corn.

Soon Grandpa and Uncle Thomas came down the field towards them. After working hard all afternoon, they were ready for a short break. They were always happy to see Grandma, and Grandpa especially enjoyed it when the grandchildren came with her out to the field.

If they had a hay rack, Grandpa and Uncle Thomas usually sat on the back of it while they ate their lunch. The children and the dog would run and play games, being careful not to stray too far from the adults. They had been warned about little children getting lost in fields, and they knew that it was dangerous.

When they grew tired of playing, they crawled up on the hay rack to rest and sit beside Grandpa and Uncle Thomas, and visit with them while they ate their lunch. Sometimes Uncle Thomas had coffee, or sometimes he preferred the Kool-Aid, but no matter how hot it was, Grandpa always had his afternoon coffee.

All too soon, lunch was over and Grandpa and Uncle Thomas announced that they had to get back to work. The children helped pack up the wrappers and napkins and jumped off the hay rack into the field.

They said good-bye because they knew that they would be leaving for home long before Grandpa and Uncle Thomas finished their work in the fields. They started walking back to the farmhouse as the sounds of the tractors faded away into the distance.

Little did the children know that in their future they would experience "dinner" as a fancy restaurant meal in the evening and lunch as a quick meal around noon before an afternoon meeting. In that context, lunch as they had shared it on the farm no longer existed. Only if they closed their eyes and thought back to those summer treks to the field could they remember what Grandma's doughnuts tasted like. And maybe, just maybe, if they listened real hard, they still might hear the sounds of tractors in the distance.

The farm near Jackson

MicheLe Larson, who grew up in Windom and graduated from high school there in 1982, spent many happy childhood hours on her grandparents' Jackson farm. She now lives in Chicago

Picking Potatoes
by MicheLe L. Larson

Grandpa was a farmer. He spent all his life in southwestern Minnesota, farming the same land his ancestors had farmed. But more than that, Grandpa was a gardener, and his favorite crop was potatoes. He loved planting them, he liked picking them, he enjoyed peeling them, and always--he took pleasure in eating them. He took a special delight in his grandchildren when they too liked to eat lots of potatoes.

Grandpa was very particular about when the potatoes got planted. He was a religious, pious man who looked to God and the Bible for all the guiding principles of his life. But when it came to planting potatoes, he also went by the moon and the calendar. Somehow there was a formula about the moon's cycle in relation to Easter that determined the appropriate time for planting potatoes. Once Grandpa decided when this would be, everyone helped-- Mom, Dad, and the grandchildren.

The children were given ice cream pails filled with seed potatoes (wedges of potatoes with the appropriate number of eyes), and they would walk down their rows and place the wedges a few inches apart. If their pails got empty, Grandpa was always ready to fill them up again. Every year, Grandpa insisted that they plant three kinds of potatoes: red ones, white ones, and russets. Grandpa and Grandma said russet potatoes were the best for making lefse, and they always wanted to be sure there were plenty of good russets for that.

Like everything else in the garden and fields, the potatoes grew all summer. In early summer, the first potatoes, though small, would be ready to eat. It was common to see Grandpa wearing his old straw hat and sitting at the picnic table peeling large pans of potatoes he had brought in from the garden. This was a ritual he enjoyed all through the summer, although occasionally, if it was too hot outside, you would find him sitting on a stool in the kitchen with his pan of potatoes. Grandma was thankful for this since she didn't really like to peel potatoes.

Sometime in October, Grandpa would decide it was time to harvest potatoes. Everyone always hoped for a warm, sunny Saturday afternoon, but often the sky filled with dark gray-blue clouds as the wind blew blustery promises of winter. Grandpa, Uncle Thomas, and sometimes Dad, would plow up the potatoes so that they lay on top of the soil. Then Grandpa hooked up his little trailer to the small John Deere lawn tractor and drove down to the potato patch. Mom, Dad, and the grandchildren followed him with several empty pails. Everyone took a pail and walked down a row collecting potatoes.

The children enjoyed picking potatoes because it was the one time they were allowed to play in the dirt. Their hands got dirty, their shoes got dirty, and sometimes, their pants got dirty if they lost their balance in the loose soil and fell down. The children also enjoyed turning it into a contest about who had the largest, smallest, ugliest, or strangest potato.

As their pails got full, everyone walked back to the lawn tractor and dumped their pails into the little trailer. When the trailer was empty, the potatoes made very loud thunk, thunk, thunk noises as they hit the bottom. But the sound of potatoes being poured into the trailer grew muffled as the trailer filled. Pail after pail, row after row, potatoes were picked. Grandpa always made the children feel important and exclaimed what good workers they were as they came with their pails full. He promised that there would be "plenty of potatoes" to last through winter.

Mid-afternoon, Grandma would come out and tell everyone to come in for lunch. Mom took the children into the bathroom and tried to scrub all the dirt off their hands so they could eat. Often she used rough Lava soap, which the children didn't like. The adults drank coffee, but Grandma had hot chocolate for the children, to "warm them up" she would say. Grandma served bread, butter, and jam sandwiches and plenty of her homemade donuts.

After lunch, everyone went back to the potato patch to finish picking. They always got done before the sun went down, but the children's fingers had usually gotten cold. The little trailer was now filled with potatoes, and Dad put a board across the back end of the trailer so they wouldn't fall out.

Then came the best part--riding with Grandpa on the little lawn tractor as they pulled the potatoes up to the house! One of the children sat in Grandpa's lap, and one sat on the fender next to him. Or sometimes, if there was room, the children might get to ride in the trailer with the potatoes. Grandpa started the little tractor, drove out of the potato patch, up the ditch, onto the driveway and back to the house. Mom and Dad walked behind, picking up any stray potatoes that fell out of the trailer.

At the house, the children ran inside to wash their hands and talk with Grandma, or play the piano. Their work was done. Grandpa backed the trailer up to the basement window while Dad went downstairs and took out the window. Then, with Dad working in the basement and Grandpa and Mom working outside, the potatoes were placed in pails, passed through the window, and dumped into the root cellar, where they would stay for the winter. When all the potatoes were safely inside the root cellar, Mom, Dad and Grandpa went in the house to visit. It had been a long, busy day, but as Grandma said, "Many hands make light work."

It wasn't just potatoes that were being cultivated; it was also good work ethics. The children were learning that you never quit until the job is done, something they later recalled as they were preparing for exams in high school and college. The children were learning that goals are achieved when everyone works together, a lesson they later demonstrated in their work lives. The children were learning that it's okay to get your hands dirty, and if you go home tired at the end of the day, it means you put in a hard day of honest work, and that's something to be proud of. Yes, it had been another good potato harvest, but it had also been another successful lesson in honing the children's work habits and preparing them for their futures.

MicheLe and her sister Christine picking potatoes

The Witch on Winter Avenue
by Julie Westrum King

Now I realize that conquering the Witch on Winter Avenue taught me a subtle lesson about the value of truth and the comfort of illusion. Just like other lessons we learn on the way from childhood to maturity, my adventure included laughter, daring, profit, and loss.

"I know where we can get some good apples," Clark said. The rest of us looked at each other, nodded, and turned back to Clark. There were four or five of us neighborhood kids who had stopped our bikes near the railroad tracks behind the Fountain Street Grocery--a favorite gathering place. None of us had any money for the penny candy or popsicles in the store. It was late summer, the fair was over, and the first day of school was just around the corner. We were hot and bored with our summer activities--so exciting in June and July, but rote and routine by now.

"Follow me!" Clark called, taking off down Fountain Street and turning right on Winter Avenue. After a block or so, he crossed to the other side of the street and stopped on the sidewalk. We didn't see any apple trees there.

A couple of kids already were shaking their heads at Clark, but I had no idea why. This was my first summer in the neighborhood because I had transferred into fourth grade at Abbott School during the middle of the previous term. I was the newest member of our gang comprised of the children of families on Second and Third Avenues. Being the newest, I was anxious to find out Clark's apple secret.

"Okay, these apples are the best, but they are guarded by a witch, and you have to be fast because she'll chase you with her broom if she catches you. Who'll go for 'em?" he asked as he pointed to her house.

Everyone was looking studiously at the sidewalk or fiddling with handlebars. Rollie contemplated the scab on his elbow, decided it wasn't ready to pick, and just scratched around it. I followed Clark's pointing finger to the lush apple tree peeking out behind my great-grandmother's house across the street.

Maude Johnson was a feisty little woman in her early 80s at the time. It was true that the best apples in the neighborhood grew on two trees in her backyard. Every year at Christmas there were big jars of her chunky applesauce under the tree for everyone and sometimes apple butter too. If dinner at Grandma's didn't end with apple pie, we were all disappointed.

The windows of her dining room were full of dozens of African violets; she had the magic touch with them, for sure. In her formal parlor, the stiff furniture was festooned with handmade doilies, both tatted and crocheted, and she proudly displayed souvenir pillows from Japan, Korea, New York and other exotic places where her children, grandchildren, or she had been. There was a card table set up in the parlor with a jigsaw puzzle in progress. Every time I visited, I had to put in at least one puzzle piece before Grandma would allow me to go! The puzzle table only came down on Bunco night. I loved to be there on Bunco night. The dice would rattle, the ladies would laugh, and there were wonderful smells of freshly baked pie or cake and hot coffee brewing.

When we moved to Second Avenue, Grandma was getting older, and relatives worried that she wasn't eating much. Mother, who worked full time, came up with the idea of sending me over to Grandma Johnson's for lunch a few days a week, as she put it to Grandma, "to keep an eye on Julie." Little did Grandma know, I was the one keeping an eye on her.

My father, Lyle Westrum, being the oldest grandchild, was always Grandma's favorite (according to him), and he made visits to her as often as he could. One day I went along with Dad. I'd never been to visit Grandma with just Dad, and I was in for a real surprise. We sat around chatting for a bit, and then Grandma said, "Did you bring it, Gus? I'm almost out."

"Sure did, " he replied. My mouth fell open as I watched my father pull a quart of Wild Turkey out of his coat pocket. He walked over to Grandma's dresser, opened the bottom drawer and switched the full bottle for a nearly empty one hidden under her needlework. This revelation bowled me over much more that the sexy romance novels I had found in her bedroom. I was lucky enough to have this surprising Irish great-grandmother in my life until I was 16.

So that hot August day, as I looked across Winter Avenue, I stifled a gasp of surprise (or was it outrage at Grandma Johnson being characterized as a witch?), cleared my throat and spoke up. “I’ll get us some apples.”

Nancy, the only other girl there, punched Clark hard in the arm. “You should go. It was your idea.”

“Hey, if Julie wants to try it, let her.” He chuckled darkly, and the other boys followed suit.

“I can do it. Let me try,” I insisted, enjoying being in the spotlight and sure of my success. Not waiting for an answer, I set my kickstand and stepped off the curb to cross the street. I heard one or two quick intakes of breath behind me as I marched resolutely down the driveway toward the tree.

I noticed Grandma Johnson standing at the kitchen window by the sink. I nodded at her slightly and continued to the back of the house, out of sight of the gang across the street. She met me at the back door.

“Hi, Grandma! Can I get some apples for me and my friends?”

“Sure, Honey. Careful on the ladder. Are you comin’ over for lunch tomorrow?”

I answered affirmatively, waved at her, and headed to the tree. My friends could see me now as I set up the stepladder, made a pouch out of the bottom of my shirt and filled it was a half-dozen of the best apples within my reach. I returned the stepladder to the back porch, gave Grandma a final wave, and then sprinted around the corner of the house, down the drive, and across the street. I quickly dumped the apples into my bike basket, jumped on, and took off yelling, “Meet up at my house!” over my shoulder.

I tore up the alley and skidded to a stop in my own back yard, followed quickly by the rest of the gang. All of us were laughing, and a glimmer of respect shone in the eyes of the boys as I passed out the apples.

We sank into the grass, munching the sun-warmed apples as our breathing quieted. Although I intended to keep up the "brave Julie" routine, I couldn't do it.

"You know, that lady isn't really a witch." I had everyone's attention at that. Slowly, I scanned their faces and continued, "She's my great-grandma." Everyone looked incredulous. I could have stopped at that, but again, I couldn't help myself. "She'd give you apples if you ask, but she just doesn't like it when you steal them."

That did it. Not only did I show up the boys and puncture their fantasy, I also called them thieves. Each of them finished his apple, let the core fly across the alley, remounted his bike and rode away. Nancy gave me a look and followed the boys.

Even though we all met up later for our nightly game of Free the People (our neighborhood version of Kick the Can), and continued to be playmates until our family moved away three years later, there was a difference. Since the day I exposed the Witch on Winter Avenue, our group dynamic was permanently changed, however slightly. I guess some of the magic went out of the neighborhood that day.

My great-grandma Maude Johnson

Julie Westrum King, who grew up in several southern Minnesota communities including Albert Lea, Faribault and New Ulm, taught high school speech and English in Wisconsin. She now lives in Mankato, where she teaches English at East High School.

Memories of My Sister Joanne
by Marian Westrum

The day my sister Joanne was born, I came down with German measles in my seventh grade arithmetic class so I was sent home. The nurse who came to take care of Mom and Joanne acquired an additional patient, and I was teased for years about being so excited to finally have a sister that I broke out in spots.

I had two brothers before I was 3 years old. I loved them dearly, and we had a lot of fun playing together, but I had always thought it would be fun to have a sister too. I had to wait until I was 13 years old before my sister was born.

The night before, without any explanation, we three older kids were told that our Aunt Hannah wanted us to spend the night at her house. We obediently walked over there and stayed the night. The next morning Dad called us at Aunt Hannah's and said, "On your way to school, stop at home and see your little sister." We stopped to see her, and noticed how tiny she was with lots of black hair. Later that dark hair came out, and she was a blonde all her life.

I had always loved to play with my dolls, and now I would have a real live doll to play with. My dad called us all together and said, "What shall we call this little girl?" I suggested "Joanne," and he even asked me how to spell it. My brother Ray suggested "Barbara," so she became Joanne Barbara. Years later my brother Forry, who was 9 years old at the time, told me that all he could think about was now we had another mouth to feed. Of course, Joanne was adored and spoiled by her older siblings. By the time Joanne was 2 years old, she loved to walk down and watch brother Ray's rabbit in its cage in our backyard.

In ninth grade sewing class we had an assignment to make a dress for a large doll. I received permission to make a dress for my 2-year-old sister instead. The dress won a prize and was displayed in the hall showcase. Over the years I took pleasure in making sure Joanne had lovely dresses for important occasions. I made the dress and panties she wore to her first day of kindergarten because our mom was busy with little brother Keith by then. Joanne's seventh birthday was a month before I was married, and I bought her a party dress and gave her a birthday party. Years later I made her beautiful white satin wedding dress.

Joanne did not like to be teased. I told her she couldn't have a church wedding because I hadn't had one, and she didn't realize I was teasing. Finally I said, "You have whatever kind of wedding you want, and she had a lovely wedding at the Calvary Baptist Church in Albert Lea on June 6, when the irises were in full bloom. I was matron of honor, and her friend was bridesmaid, and our dresses, which I made, complemented the flowers. Mine was yellow, and her friend's dress was orchid.

Joanne and her husband had a son and three daughters, including twins, and they lived in Owatonna. We were always the best of friends, going back and forth for visits with our respective families, and her son was only about two years younger than my daughter Julie.

With her children raised, Joanne contracted breast cancer, and at age 68, after a strong round of chemotherapy, she died of a heart attack. Her husband died two months later. It was so difficult to lose that baby sister I wanted so much and loved so dearly, and I couldn't understand why she had to die so young. Her four brothers and I, along with her four children, will always miss her and treasure the memory of Joanne.

Joanne Porter age 10

Marian Westrum lives in Albert Lea. She has an adult son and daughter and two grandchildren. Her daughterJulie wrote the previous story.

Growing Up at the State School in Owatonna
by Marcella Brown Roseland

I was around 8 years old in 1935 when I went to live in the orphanage at Owatonna. In the depths of the Great Depression, my mom and a baby died in childbirth, leaving my dad alone to raise six children near Brainerd. A man who was widowed had a very tough time in those days because if he hired a woman to come in to take care of his kids, gossip about impropriety would fly around the community, making his life difficult.

Dad thought he solved that problem when he brought a wonderful elderly Negro nanny from the South to care for us, and we loved her dearly. However, when the Ku Klux Klan came over to our house and burned crosses on the lawn, Dad got scared and had to send the nanny away. He had no way to take care of us.

I was the third oldest of three boys and three girls. We stayed in an orphanage in the Twin Cities for about six months until they found room for all of us at the Minnesota State School in Owatonna, and I lived there seven years. Over the years I have heard negative stories from some former State School kids, but my experience was positive, and I have only good memories of the years I spent there.

Shortly after my arrival, I was in the hospital for over four months with rheumatic fever. I had always loved to read, but after I got out of the hospital I wasn't allowed to read much because I'd had terrible eye problems from the illness, and they were afraid I would hurt my eyes again if I read. I was about 9 years old, and this restriction set up a conflict because I was being deprived of something I really liked to do, and I was strong-minded.

I wanted to work in the library, and the librarian said she didn't know if it would hurt me to work there or not. She told me that I should damage a book. Then, when they went to ask the librarian for advice about what to do about the damaged book, she would tell them that I had to work in the library to pay for the book. She and I giggled about this.

I feel that this librarian did something to enable me to pursue my interest, and she helped me accomplish something by helping me learn to work with books. I indexed and fixed books, but I didn't read while I worked. I dreamed of becoming a librarian, and while this never happened, I resumed my reading after awhile, and I continue to be an avid reader. Sometimes I read a book a day, and I have passed my love of reading to my children and grandchildren.

Other adults at the State School also affected my life in a positive way. My cottage matron, Miss Conway, was extremely easy going and kind. When she moved on, Mrs. Schaeffer replaced her. Since we girls were all getting a little older, Mrs. Schaeffer felt she needed to enforce some rules.

One day when we were about 12, my friends and I decided we were angry with Mrs. Schaeffer, and we were going to beat her up. As we were rounding up weapons like hair brushes and dust pans, she heard about the revolution and came to our door. She told us that if we put our weapons down she would be glad to talk to us, and if we were still mutinous after our chat, we could go ahead with the beating.

We sat down for a visit, and that's when I decided that I should behave myself. Mrs. Schaeffer explained to the four of us why she had been laying down some rules. She said she wanted us to grow up to be real ladies who know how to talk respectfully, how to keep a clean house, and how to do our work.

She wasn't mean, but we had at first thought some of the things she wanted us to do were far-fetched. After our talk we decided not to beat up on her because we realized that she was teaching us to get along in the world. We put away our dust pans and other weapons and agreed to get along.

Even after that truce, we weren't always perfectly behaved. One time my friend Mary Jane and I were punished for some misdeed--I don't remember what. We were allowed to go out and play, but we were forbidden to talk. While we were outside jumping rope, the minister came along and greeted us. He tried to exchange small talk, but we merely shook our heads and smiled.

Finally, after a lot of talking on his part and silence on our parts, he asked if we were being punished, and when we nodded yes, he said he'd come by sometime when we could talk, and he went on his way smiling. The matron must have seen what happened because she called us in and told us that we could always speak to the minister, even when we were being punished. Then she laughed and lifted our talking ban.

Mrs. Schaeffer went to bat for me when I wanted to go to a dance. We had a chalkboard where we received checks for bad behavior and for failing to do our work properly. Some inspectors gave me a check for not dusting under my bed, thus making me ineligible to attend the dance. I went upstairs and talked to the girls, but did not redo the dusting. When the inspector rechecked, she said it was better and asked why hadn't I done it right the first time.

My friends verified that I had done nothing to improve the dusting, and Mrs. Schaeffer came along and told the checker that it was okay to take my word for it. Then she erased not only my last demerit check on the board, but all the checks, and she said I could go to the dance after all. That she stood up for me really made me feel important. Mrs. Schaeffer became my lifelong friend, and when I grew up and had children of my own, she visited my family at our home frequently.

I must have had a reputation for getting my way. A man at a reunion came up to me and asked, "Are you still a little stinker like you was at the orphanage?" He must have heard some of those stories.

Before my mother died and after I moved to the orphanage, I always knew I was loved. I bonded with Miss Woodfill, Miss Conway and Mrs. Schaeffer, who were my substitute mothers. I was encouraged to write to my dad and cousins near Brainerd, Pillager and Motley so we stayed in touch.

Mrs. Schaefer asked every month if I'd written to my family. She would greet me at the door and ask if I had homework, and she would help me and the other girls if we needed it. My sister Marie, who was about five years older, looked out for me and my other siblings, and we all stayed together because none of us was adopted.

I made it through some pretty tough times in my early childhood, but I firmly believe that what I learned at the orphanage in Owatonna has helped me lead a successful life. I learned to speak well, to work hard, to be polite and to appreciate what I have in life. I learned those lessons and they served me well, and I will always speak positively of my days at the Minnesota State School in Owatonna.

The Minnesota State School in Owatonna

Marcella Brown Roseland lives in Owatonna, and she enjoys reading.

Cora Conklin
by Timothy Conklin

Cora Conklin, my grandmother, was a woman of the Twentieth Century; her life spanned it entirely. When she was born, William McKinley was President of the United States, and Queen Victoria sat on the British throne. She was 4 years old when Orville and Wilbur Wright launched their *Flyer* above the dunes of Kitty Hawk, North Carolina. She told me that she screamed for her sister Virgie and ran to the house when the first plane she ever saw flew over their farm sometime before World War I.

Cora was the second of eleven children born to Edward and Molly Hubbard. She was born near Hubbard, Iowa and lived near Indianola and Austin before her family settled on a place near Wells. For Cora, Wells meant home, and she referred to her family, the farm, and all those family reunions as taking place, "over home."

In 1918 Cora attended Simpson College in Indionola, Iowa for a term. Inside her textbook, *Domestic Science, Principles and Application*, she wrote her name, and throughout the book she wrote sparse notes. One note reads, "War ended. November 11, 1918. Peace treaty signed at 2:00. Algebra class Thursday."

She was just 20 years old in 1919 when she married Melvin Conklin from Indianola, and the couple moved to a farm of their own near Lansing, Minnesota. In 1925 she gave birth to Muriel, and three years later their son Dale was born. When Cora was 30, she was working on a farm with her husband and taking care of two little ones when the stocks crashed and the U.S. entered the Great Depression.

Cora was a farm wife and a farm mother, and she made sure there was always food on the table for those kids of hers. She was resourceful, and she knew it was up to her to help provide for her family. One year she raised turkeys. She slaughtered and butchered them and packed them into barrels to ship to Chicago. Cora made $400 on those turkeys, and with that money, she went out and bought a Ford Model A--black, of course.

In the early 1940s, Cora's family moved off the farm and into a house in Austin. They took in a 7-year-old girl named Alice Dahl, who made her home with them. Cora always worked hard. She took in borders, she took in ironing, and she baby-sat for the neighbors. She cooked and washed dishes for the Elks, the Eagles and the Country Club. She clerked at Averbrooks and Wallace's on Main Street in their yard goods department, and sometimes her grandchildren would visit her there after school.

Cora loved to cook, and I remember her tarts that she made with leftover pie dough and her own homemade apple jelly. She said that the secret to her flaky crust was Fluffo brand shortening. I don't know about the shortening, but I do know that as a little boy I would be surrounded by grandmotherly love whenever I went to her house. Whether it was her greeting to me, "Hey Barney Google," or her homemade apple jelly tarts, I felt loved.

She loved to knit and tat. Some of the grandkids remember the wonders of her linen closet and how every sheet and pillowcase was perfectly ironed, folded and stacked. Whenever they slid down her stairs, those kids made way too much noise.

When I was 5 or so, Grandma was watching me at her home while my parents were at work and my sisters and brother were at school. On those long, quiet afternoons, Grandma would sit with me on her front step there at her home at 510 2nd Street Southeast and together we would watch the trains load up boxcars on the tracks behind the neighbor's house across the street. And she would say to me, "You know, Barney Google? Someday you and me, we're gonna climb aboard one of those trains and we're gonna go."

Of course, my 5-year-old brain was fired with thoughts of adventure, but beneath that was almost a sense of wonder that my 68-year-old grandmother would even say such a thing as, "We're gonna climb aboard and we're gonna go." And I think that more than just stirring her grandkid's imagination, she was confiding something to me about her own desire to take a journey and leave her mundane world filled with its responsibilities and travel, footloose and fancy free--just for a bit. Just enough to get away for awhile then come home. It was revolutionary talk coming from my grandmother, and I always remembered.

In her last years, she lived with Alzheimer's disease that gradually took her out of our world. But she always seemed comfortable, cheerful, and content with the care she received from the wonderful staff of St. Mark's Nursing Home.

She lived in three centuries and died in 2002. When she was born, mankind hadn't yet learned to fly. When she died, we had flown through space and put people on the moon. But when I think of travel, I think of those trains, Grandma, and I think you have finally climbed aboard.

Timothy Conklin graduated from Austin High School, served in the Peace Corps in Nepal, and returned to Nepal to work as a technical trainer. He teaches English at the University of British Columbia in Vancouver.

A Busy Day for a Farm Family
by Elizabeth (Betty) James Stoesz

When I was growing up, we lived on a farm halfway between Elko and Webster. We got up early and worked hard every day, but occasionally we would enjoy a special treat-- a trip to town.

Once in awhile we went to Faribault or Northfield to buy clothing or other things we needed, traveling in our Ford Touring Car. It had side curtains that snapped down when it rained. Every trip was a different experience and very exciting because we didn't go very often. We drove the county dirt road out to Lyndale Highway, which was gravel. Tires were not what they are today. They had a tube liner filled with air, and we always had several blowouts on the road. Dad would have to pull over to the side, take the tire off, remove the tube, and get out the patching material, which everyone carried in those days. With a small scraper he would rough up the area around the hole, then glue the patch on. He put back the tube into the tire and then put it on the wheel so he could pump air back into it with a hand pump.

On one of our trips, we had several flats, and it took us a long time to get to Faribault--a distance of about 25 miles. We had to eat before we could watch a circus parade. We enjoyed that as Dad went to a bakery and bought Danish rolls and white bread. We always had homemade bread and cakes at home because Mother baked twice a week.

We had carried cold tea and lemonade with us, and Dad bought Van Camp pork and beans and bologna for sandwiches. We thought it was a great treat to eat all that store-bought food, and we took our feast to Central Park and had a picnic. Then we went to watch the circus parade.

The band came first, followed by the animal wagons with lions, tigers and other animals. There were lots of clowns and fancy dressed ladies on decorated horses. A giraffe or two were followed by the elephants--one in front of the other holding on to the tails. It was a full day by the time we got home.

We had to change clothes and do the evening chores of milking thirty cows by hand and watering all our livestock. Meanwhile, Mom and one of us girls got busy cooking supper. Our suppers usually consisted of leftover fried potatoes, some meat and vegetables from our garden, and finally fruit sauce or cornstarch pudding or Jell-O for dessert. The Jell-O had been hanging in a pail in the well to thicken because we had no refrigerator or ice to chill it. It never did get really solid.

Our well had an iron pump, and that is where we got our water. We carried one pailful at a time into the house--a pail for drinking and another for cooking. We had a cistern under the house that caught the rainwater, and we used that water for hand washing, bathing, and scrubbing floors--but not for consumption. We drank well water. When it was time to get cleaned up for bed, we took salt and soda and a glass of water and went out on the lawn to brush our teeth, next to the outhouse.

Our bed consisted of a straw mattress on wire springs and sheets made of flour sacks sewn together. After our busy and memorable day in town, we slept well anticipating the next busy day on the farm.

Betty James Stoesz lives in Prescott, Arizona.

Back on the Farm in Raymond
by Simon Zimmer

I was born on September 1, 1921 at Clara City. My folks owned a 320-acre farm at Raymond, so that's where I grew up.

Truly times were very different then, and I remember cheaper groceries, gas at 12 cents a gallon, hogs selling for 2 cents a pound, and corn was 3 cents a bushel. Movies cost 10 cents, and a hair cut and a shave cost two bits. I'm sure the younger generation has a hard time believing such figures.

My father was a horse farmer so our barn always held a good number of horses. Usually we had 12-14 milk cows and young stock. Milking always was done by hand, although a few farmers got milking machines in later years. We usually had about 100 head of hogs, maybe 40 head of sheep, some chickens and some years turkeys or ducks and a few geese.

We lived three miles from Raymond and 2.7 miles from a country school. I started at country school, then after one year went to Raymond Public School and then went back to the country school for sixth and seventh grades--then back to the public school for eighth grade. Work on the farm was too important so high school was out of the question for many farm boys, including me.

Winters were cold so we wore two pairs of pants over long johns, two pairs of socks, and two pairs of mittens and our coats as we walked three miles to school. We seldom got a ride so we were hardy farm boys, all bundled up. Compared to the winter clothes they sell today, all our clothes were flimsy, so we had to walk briskly to stay warm.

I remember well when Charles Lindbergh made his solo flight across the huge water nonstop to Paris in 1927. That sure made the news, and Lindbergh was a hero for our times. With no daily newspaper or television, we got our news from a battery radio and a weekly paper. Honestly, Lindberg's flight was bigger news back in '27 than the moon landing was in 1969.

In 1929 we were blessed with Northern State electric power, and there was light that made it feel like a brand new world. No more lanterns or dim kerosene lamps. A 200-watt yard light truly made a difference; at last you could see where you were going. For several years, due to hard times, our current was shut off during the summer and turned back on starting in October.

We had a severe drought that lasted from 1931-1934. With no rain there were no crops, no hay, no pastures and even the wells went dry. We hauled water from Prinsburg, a neighboring town some ten miles away. Some feed was shipped in, but that didn't last, and cattle and hogs had to be shipped to markct. The price of animals many times didn't pay for the freight. In the Dakotas, ranchers sold everything and moved away. The countryside looked brown as a desert.

In 1935 things began to improve, and 1936 was good again. Since then we have had some very wet years, but never those terrible dust storms. In those years, farmers never received aid of any kind. Today it's always government checks for everything. Many people left their farms and never returned, so it was amazing that we made it through. Those were mighty tough years and certainly not very healthy ones either.

So far I've given you some history, but now I'll give you a month-by-month summary of what we did on the farm where I grew up.

In January it was cold so mostly we did routine chores. We got up early, fed cattle, milked 12-15 cows by hand and then separated the milk, and finished feeding the young stock, horses, hogs sheep or whatever we had at the time. We went to the house for Mom's good breakfast and did some more chores, cleaned barns, and let cows and horses outside to the water tank for a good drink.

We had a wind-powered well and never running water in the barns. Running water came much later. In winter we chopped a lot of wood. We took milk and cream and eggs to town and picked up groceries. The housewives did much cooking and baking on cook stoves fired with corn cobs and wood. They had to wash clothes and hang them on lines outside, where they froze stiff, or inside the house if it was especially cold.

February work was much the same with shoveling snow and doing everyday chores. In March we started doing repair work. We shelled seed corn, graded it, and sacked it for planting. Grains had to be cleaned, and maybe we shelled corn for feed to grind in town to make hog feed.

In April spring field work would start, and naturally the weather was much warmer. Maybe we'd haul hay from far out in the fields, maybe haul some grains to the elevator to sell. There would always be weather delays with planting to harvesting to fall work.

May was corn-planting time. We had two-horse, two-row planters. We always used a check wire planting corn; that way we could cultivate to keep fields clean. Today farmers don't cultivate but spray corn, beans and small grains. We even hand picked the fields for bad weeds, and that was time consuming each year.

In June we cultivated corn and beans and cut and hauled hay. We started to harvest grain in July, first cutting with horses or grain binder, shocking bundles of oats or wheat, which was a hot, tedious job too. If we didn't shock them and stand them up, they would get wet lying on the ground.

August was threshing time. Dad had the thresher, and threshing bees took place with four or five neighbors. This lasted some three weeks with rain delays. We harvested more hay, and some farmers raised flax, and it was a few more days of pitching bundles in the thresher.

In September we plowed and harvested grain fields. I did a lot of plowing with three horses on a sulky plow. As I grew up, I graduated to five or six horses on the two-bottom gang plow. If you had a good lead team to lead the way, you got a lot more area covered in a day.

October brought a change in temperature and shorter days. There was corn to cut with a binder for winter feed. And the corn husking started, a slow job of pulling ears off stalks and peeling the husk and putting or throwing them into the wagon. Each man would take two rows at a time. The smart horses knew how to keep pulling the wagon along. This was a slow, long, drawn-out job, and you could run into some cold days and moisture. Sometimes it would even snow.

You unloaded at noon and again in the evening. Shoveling a big load of ear corn in cribs was no easy task. Unless you have done it, you have no idea of the backbreaking job it was. When you came home from the field it was pretty dark, and you still had to do all your normal chores. After supper there was that big load of corn to shovel yet. Sleep did wonders to restore a guy to dig in and get busy again the next day.

By November there was lots of corn left in the field yet, and colder and snowy days slowed you down. With shorter days, you continued to pick corn but struggled to keep up with getting other jobs done during the short days. When it was done, you were so happy. Yes, it always came to an end, and cattle could be turned out to feed on the stalks and whatever.

By December, the field work would be all finished, but there would always be livestock to tend and more chores to do on the farm. Farming was a 365-day-a-year job, without vacations.

Later tractors did more of the hard work on farms, and the horses became a lost art for most farmers. I always liked to work and drive horses. Certainly it was a lot less stressful. Slowly the horses became unnecessary, and their worth became less and less. I left the farm in 1950, and my prize teams of sorrels sold for $150. A horse jockey thought he could buy them for $25, but they were my pride and joy. Horses were dependable, never failed to start up like tractors did, and they were smart animals. Some farmers would haul their milk and cream to town, and if a guy had a few too many drinks, the saloon keeper would put him in his wagon and send the horses home. Naturally they made it, and the wife had to tend to the team and take the guy inside.

We used to have snowstorms that lasted several days, and we would have to rig a wire or rope to feel our way out to the barns. Lots of people lost their lives in severe snowstorms. Once you got blown around, it was easy to lose direction, get lost, and freeze to death. Those drifts could pile up high, and they were hard so you could walk on them. After the storms, you needed energy as there was much work shoveling, and then more drifting and more shoveling. Cars couldn't go, so again those dependable horses came through. Bob sleds were quite popular in those days, and all the city kids would ride on their the runners or in the box.

We usually burned corn cobs in our heating stoves. Then all the woodcutting had to be done for the winter season. Lots of logs needed splitting, a great cold weather job. We would take some 500 pounds of wheat and rye to the feed mill at Renville some ten miles away. That would last all winter long and would be baked into mighty tasty breads and food.

The women played a huge part in the life on the farm--baking, sewing, washing, and cooking all day. Remember, all the modern things came much later, so women had no washers, dryers, freezers, refrigerators, water heaters, mixers, indoor plumbing, or any other appliances that would make life easier. Everything had to be done the hard way.

We had no milking machines, snow blowers or any of these modern conveniences. We couldn't jump in the car and go, but our legs could help us get anywhere. Today life on the farm is so different with nice modern homes, three car garages, and time to attend games, movies and dances. There are no 20 below zero trips to the outhouse, huddling around the kitchen stove to keep warm, or outdoor clotheslines. Just think of the super warm clothing and boots we have today.

In the old days, people just didn't have all the choices and conveniences we have today. I'm amazed that people survived, and I wonder what the next 100 years will hold for us. We've seen so many changes of direction. We don't know what the future holds, and it's best we don't know.

Simon Zimmer retired from farming in 1950 and moved to Willmar, where he did carpentry and custodial work for the school district. He and his wife Gloria have three children and six grandchildren.

The Games We Used to Play
by Carol Keech Malzahn

•Red Rover, Red Rover, Send Kathy Right Over! •Lemonade •Pump Pump Pull Away •Starlight Moonlight, Hope to See the Ghost Tonight •Spin the Bottle •Jump Rope, •Higher and Higher •Post Office, •Freeze Tag •Statue, •Mummy, •Kick the Can, •Clap In-Clap Out, •One Potato, Two Potato • I See Something R-e-d, R-e-d, R-e-d. I See Something R-e-d. Guess What it Can Be.

These are some of the games that kept us occupied while growing up in Minnesota, long before we ever heard the word "computer." A laptop was where we sat to have our hurts mended and our tears wiped.

When the Keech, Lindquist, Siem and Olson families gathered on a Saturday night for the adults to play cards, there were eight adults and as many as sixteen children present! (More if we had cousins staying over with us.) No, we weren't Catholics, just careless Lutherans.

Starlight, Moonlight, Hope to See the Ghost Tonight! was the game we played after it got dark. The little kids went inside when we began this game. One person was picked to hide somewhere in the darkness, near the perimeter of the house. The rest of us would stand on the back step and chant, "One o'clock, two o'clock, three o'clock, rock. Four o'clock, five o'clock, six o'clock rock. Seven o'clock, eight o'clock, nine o'clock rock. Ten o'clock, eleven o'clock, twelve o'clock. NOON" That gave the person hiding fair warning that his or her time to find the best hiding place was half up. We continued on, chanting around the clock until we yelled out, "MIDNIGHT - *Starlight moonlight, hope to see the ghost tonight*!"

We had to run around the entire house in the darkness, anticipating someone jumping out from behind a tree or bush to catch us. We were safe if we could reach one foot back on the step before we were caught.

If you were caught, you stayed with that person and helped catch more kids until there was only one person not caught. This person was the winner. If everyone was caught, then the kid doing the most catching was the winner.

We often made up our own rules and regulations as the night progressed, accordingly to the situations that befell us. If the game was taking place at your house, you got to make up rules. That way we avoided some spats.

We would play this game for hours until we would smell a skunk, the mosquitoes would chase us inside, or our beautiful Minnesota summer night turned into a rainy night with lightning. If there wasn't lightning, we could stay outside in the rain.

Another miserable end to the game was when those "big" boys would pull a prank of some kind. The worst prank they played on us during *Starlight Moonlight* took place one unusually dark, summer night. The boys had somehow all been caught and were hiding in the darkness while all us girls were on the step chanting in our best soprano chanting voices, making up a dance routine to go with the chant, throwing in a cartwheel here and there, "One o'clock, two o'clock, three o'clock, rock" ...all the way around the clock, 24 hours. "MIDNIGHT" - *Starlight moonlight, hope to see the ghost tonight!"*

We felt afraid but knew we had to make it. At least one of us HAD to make it. It just wasn't fair when the boys won all the time. We stuck together and slowly crept around the corner into the darkness. Then, as fright overtook each of us, we broke apart and dashed around the house, each of us as fast as our legs could carry us. We were all so lucky. We all made it safely around the house! Wait a minute. None of us had even been chased!! Oh, NOW what were those boys up to?

We yelled into the darkness, "Cheaters! You broke the rules." There was no reply. We stalled a little longer, contemplating what we should do. Those boys were not coming out, and they were not making a sound no matter how much we protested that they were cheating. Like idiots, we decided to run around the house again. This time we were really scared and ran full steam, as fast as we could. Every girl for herself!

Just beyond the glow of the yard light, into the deep darkness of the front yard, plop, plop, plop. Each of us fell on top of the other--face first, bones crashing into bones, in the dewy wet grass. On the way down I felt a burning sensation across my bare knees. The boys had tied twine around a tree and were holding the other end tight, about knee height, and strung across our path. These kinds of tactics were part of their game.

We lay in a pile, whining and rubbing our sore knees. The boys walked up to us, laughing their heads off, and carefully poked us as they declared, "I caught you and you and you. Game over. We are the WINNERS." Oh how they gloated.

Clap In-Clap Out was a romantic indoor game we played upstairs in our bedrooms while our parents played cards downstairs in the dining room. Normally the object of the game was to telepathically pick the correct boy or girl, as the case might be, and sit beside him or her on the bed. A doorkeeper chose a member of the opposite sex to walk into the room and do the picking.

There was no skill involved. This game was played from the heart! If you sat beside the wrong person, everyone clapped and you had to walk out. Better luck next time! If you sat beside the "chosen one," you were supposed to kiss each other. In the case of that event actually occurring, there was, of course, much clapping, hooting and pulling of the light string off and on. I remember having to help hold an uncooperative guy down a time or two as we claimed our rightfully earned kiss!

We girls absolutely loved this game and had to BEG the boys to go along with it. Our hearts practically pounded right out of our chests in hopes of getting that first kiss.

Of course, as we got older, we realized that if the boy who sat by us was not the one we wanted to kiss, we plotted to save each other and clap even if they did pick correctly, as we never knew which boy was going to be sent in. (Especially if it was our brother. Ugh!) And we all knew who wanted to kiss whom. Eventually we just gave up choosing one girl. If the right guy came in and sat by the right girl, of course he won a kiss! Those boys had tremendous telepathy.

Although the girls loved the game, the boys were always laughing and ridiculing and hurting us. They were relentless. We ended up with more dog piles and fights on the beds than any kisses.

"What are you kids doing up there!" It was usually our dad. "Simmer down NOW or I'm going to have to come up there!"

The one major factor contributing to the end of the game was the crash of a bed breaking. That was the absolute last straw. We all had to go sit in the living room or kitchen where the parents could keep an eye on us. As you can imagine, with sixteen kids – "*The party's over. It's time to say good night.*" Not until we had "lunch" though.

The fun-loving and attractive gang of cousins back in Sveadahl--most of them. I am in the front row, second from the left.

Carol Keech Malzahn grew up in Sveadahl and now lives in Minnesota Lake. She and her husband Art enjoy small town life and being grandparents.

A Mentor for Life
by Kathy A. Megyeri

St. Olaf, a liberal arts college located 35 miles south of the Twin Cities, enrolls 3,058 students from the U.S. and from 18 foreign countries. It is probably best known for its choir, its outstanding science department, and for the high percentage of alumni who go on to attend graduate school. But interestingly enough, the most popular major selected by students is English, and that was my concentrated area of study back in the early 1960s.

One of the most treasured and lasting gifts I received from my St. Olaf education was my association with Associate Professor of English Graham S. Frear. During his career at St. Olaf (1962-1986), Professor Frear taught eighteen different courses to more than two thousand students. He worked with 409 English education supervisors, including my own cooperating teacher at North High School in Minneapolis back in 1964.

Professor Frear calculated that during his St. Olaf teaching career, he administered 6,300 exams and evaluated more than 9,500 papers, arduous tasks that most teachers dread. But more importantly, over the years, he maintained contact with his former students, and his regular correspondence has kept me in touch with campus activities and the lives of professors, classmates, and colleagues. In spite of living in Washington, D.C., I've always felt connected to the school in Minnesota. This linkage between professor and former student has served me in many ways and thus makes Professor Frear my mentor for life.

First, his tenure at St. Olaf brought me a sense of the school's institutional history that is vital to feeling connected to "place." Professor Frear is unique in that he shared in the fortunes of St. Olaf as a student, alumnus, faculty member, and emeritus professor for over sixty years.

At the time of his enrollment in 1940, the campus consisted of only eight buildings, whereas now there are forty-two. Professor Frear recounts that he was an odd Ole when he enrolled. Neither Norwegian in background nor Lutheran in faith, he says he didn't know "a synod from a fence post, had never heard of Green Lake Bible Camp or Luther's small catechism. He came to St. Olaf with only his anxiety, an old suitcase, and a check for $75 to cover his first semester's tuition."

His total year's expenses were $500, so for him, 1940 became the baseline for future lessons in the economies of inflation. He remembers scratching his name with his Ytterboe dormitory key deeply into the soft yellow brick of "Old Main," the first building on campus. This was a prophetic act because his name is still there, a sign that his ties to St. Olaf are firmly bonded.

His class enrolled 400 strong, but by commencement in 1944, it had dwindled to 26 men and 84 women. The rest, he says, were dispersed on battle and defense fronts all over the world. The cemetery east of town is the resting place of many of his mentors and classmates.

Professor Frear remembers that lights in all dormitories went out at 10:30 p.m. after devotions. Ytterboe was the one men's dorm and had no procedures for signing in or out, but in the two women's dorms, signing out was required after 7:30 p.m. Heath Creek, Norway Valley, the Ole Store, the Riverside Café, which was open all night and later changed its name to Basil's, the Ideal Café, Gates Café, the Grand and West Theaters, and those distant places like Faribault and the infamous Dundas were all parts of his college existence.

In Professor Frear's student days, folk dancing was accepted, but "dancing too close to folk was not." He remembers one professor in a heavily tinged Norwegian accent who told students in his so-called "freshman hygiene class" that dancing was the vertical expression of a horizontal desire and that students should be wary of cigarette suckers, cosmetic users, and those boozers who were losers.

Many students, like Frear, attended St. John's Lutheran Church, where First Choir, as it was then called, sang every Sunday, and its director, F. Melius Christiansen, played the organ in the balcony that "rumbled with its sublime chords of Bach." Christiansen was the acclaimed director, composer and choral arranger who founded the St. Olaf Choir in 1907 and directed it until his son took over the job in 1943.

What Professor Frear consistently transmits in his reflections on his own St. Olaf career is that "Christmen Crossmen," whether students knew it or not, was an affirmation of a long and abiding Christian tradition. When they sang both refrains, "Fram, Fram" followed by "Ja vi elsker dette landet," with pride and understanding, they realized that in spite of all the school's surface development, expansion and modification, faculty changes, program proliferations and international studies programs that would reach around the world, the school's fundamental philosophy and faith were constant.

Frear and others at the school knew that the college and the church were built on rock and for that reason remain standing. The tree-covered hill of Manitou Heights lures us graduates back to reunions, parents' days, weddings, funerals, dedications and memories of past successes and tragedies because we reconnect with influential teachers like Frear who convey a sense of the school's institutional history and values. No wonder so many graduates recall the lyrics and lovingly sing the old hymn, "Bless Be the Tie that Binds."

In addition to his knowledge and regard for St. Olaf's history, Professor Frear taught me the craft of teaching well. He convinced me that teaching is the profession that most benefits society and impacts most positively on youth. Even today, according to the Research Institute, Americans cite teachers as the greatest contributors to society, and Professor Frear personified the ideals of teaching. When I once queried him about his philosophy of teaching, he wrote me the following:

"Teaching was always my way of attempting to impact attitude and dedication more than skills. I'm certain I became a teacher largely through attempting to do what I would have wanted done with me as a student. The teachers I remember were the ones who conveyed a sense of purpose and enthusiasm more than those who were centered on subject matter."

So during my own 34-year career of teaching secondary English, I attempted to follow Professor Frear's example and convey a sense of purpose and enthusiasm. Whether or not I was as successful remains to be judged, but I tried to follow his example.

Another lesson I hold dear is that Professor Frear taught me to write. My desk drawer still holds term papers dated "fall, 1963," with lengthy comments scribbled on them, so I know he not only read the papers but cared enough to note areas I could have pursued in more depth, suggested another book I might wish to read, and posted a compliment or two that made me want to please him even more on the next assignment. Because of his encouragement and knowledge, I have never feared editorial criticism when I submitted work for publication. Because Professor Frear still writes to me and offers to critique my magazine and book submissions, I'm motivated to continue pursuing a craft that was honed in his English classes back in the '60s.

My fourth lesson is that Professor Frear taught me to live a worthy life. Now that we are both retired, we are coping with a new phase of existence so he encourages me to continue the art of creativity and personal growth. Although he's been a widower for four years, has sold his home, auctioned away most valuables, dispersed many treasures to his children, and lives in a Northfield retirement complex with his cat, he avoids the sing-alongs, the group calisthenics, the old Doris Day movies and jigsaw puzzles. Instead, he cooks familiar foods in his worn-out, old pots and pans for family and friends. He voraciously reads and writes to old students like me to share news of school and friends and to offer his comments on current events and world affairs.

He recently bought a seat at the new Guthrie Theater in Minneapolis in memory of his wife, Helen, and he wrote and published a book of poems in memory of her. He breakfasts regularly with old faculty colleagues and teaching fellows from St. Olaf. He paints landscapes from photos he took during his trips to Ireland with students years ago and hangs his paintings in the halls of his retirement complex. He's tracking down his many contributed box collages that hang in homes and art galleries to make a photo record of them for family and friends.

Most importantly, he still teaches. This semester, he's instructing an Irish Literature class for the Elder Collegium that meets in his retirement home. In recognition of his continued teaching acumen, many people enrolled, but he had to hold class size at twenty because of the constraints of materials and room size. My own retirement days pale beside his active and creative life.

What he doesn't realize is that I've kept his correspondence throughout the years, and I've begun to compile paragraphs and tidbits I want to hold on to and perhaps publish after he's lost to us.

When I mailed him a clipping about Gordon Parks' latest book, he wrote back:

"I remember nominating Gordon Parks for an Honorary Doctorate at St. Olaf and reading the citation before the crowd. College President Sidney Rand was so impressed with him that he invited him back to campus, but Parks was making a movie at the time and had to return to New York. But I stood with him in his suite at the top of the St. Paul Radisson Hotel, and he took me to the windows and said, 'Those are the streets where I came from and wrote about in my book, A Choice of Weapons.' That's when, he said, he chose the pen over the switchblade and became a writer." What treasured memories Graham Frear shares with us correspondents.

Professor Graham Frear's generosity is noteworthy. He nominated me for a St. Olaf Distinguished Alumnae Award in 1995, and as a lowly teacher who really hadn't accomplished anything spectacular, I was honored to receive it at the spring commencement ceremonies that year because Frear had bothered to convince the Board of Governors that I was worthy of the award.

I remember feeling so proud until I returned to my own classes the following Monday morning. In 95-degree temperatures, since the air conditioning system was broken, I was explaining to my sleepy and hot class the metaphor of "rosy-fingered dawn" in Homer's *Odyssey* when one of the students asked, "Why do we have to know this stuff?" For a moment, I wondered too until I recalled Frear's characterization of the profession.

"Teaching is a good way to make a living. Not only does one enjoy the process itself (how lovely the sound of one's own voice), but it's like being a 'doorkeeper in the house of the Lord,' which is authoritatively stated to be better than sitting in the seats of scornful."

May every student today have the good fortune I have had to connect with a favorite teacher/mentor....one who embodies an institution's history, who perhaps influences a vocational choice, who serves as a model for life-affirming experiences, who models retirement in such worthy style, and, most importantly, serves as a cheerleader for the rest of one's life. It's the closest one can come to achieving immortality, so I hope part of Graham Frear's legacy will be that he personified the best of Minnesota.

Pofessor Graham S. Frear
St. Olaf College

Kathy Megyeri, a Washington D.C. retired English teacher, is an education consultant and writer whose contributions can be found in Chicken Soup and every volume of Minnesota Memories, the book series she co-founded in 2001. Professor Frear, the subject of this story, has also been a regular contributor, and two of his stories can be found in this volume. Kathy can be reached at Megyeri@juno.com.

The Impact of a Minnesota Town
by Kathy A. Megyeri

Owatonna, a town of 20,000 persons founded in 1854, brags of its quality of life and claims that it is a place where "progress and history entwine." What was never obvious to me until my later years is the profound influence that growing up in Owatonna had on my life. First of all, it gave me a life-long fascination with Native American Indians.

Even "Minnesota"—the land of 10,000 lakes--is a word given to us by Algonquian-speaking Ojibwas, so it should be no surprise to anyone that an Indian in full dress regalia was Owatonna High School's mascot. As a child, I was steeped in the local lore of Chief Wabena, who encountered a particularly brutal winter during which famine threatened his tribe. Owatonna, his beautiful daughter, grew ill and was carried from the Minnesota River southward to the curing water the chief's grandfather had told him of. Princess Owatonna drank the water and recovered, and townspeople say her kindly spirit still hovers near that spot. A statue of the Indian maiden stands only a few blocks from my childhood home near the curative powers of that mineral spring. It's a place that the Chamber of Commerce advertises where "travelers can pause in the beautiful valley to drink long and often of the water."

Photo courtesy of Shot in the Dark Photography, Owatonna

Even though I had student-taught at North High School in Minneapolis where many Native American students attended, and I frequently visited Pipestone, where peace pipes are fashioned out of the area's red clay, my knowledge of Native American culture was seriously inadequate, perhaps because I had so stereotyped this group and ignored their contribution to history.

More than two million American Indians exist in almost 846 tribes throughout the U.S. (the largest being Navajo), but perhaps we've erased this minority group from our consciousness because their life expectancy is still only 49 years, and they suffer from alcoholism, fetal alcohol syndrome, non consensual sterilization of both men and women, an appallingly high child and teen suicide rate, dismal employment opportunities on and off the reservation, intense community and intrapersonal conflicts that have robbed them of much of their strength, and their contributions to society are largely ignored.

At the start of my teaching career, not one of my students knew that the word "squaw" came from the Narragansett tribe meaning "woman," that without Sacajawea, the first woman to cross the Rocky Mountains, the entire Northwest Territory would not have been opened, and that the Cherokee alphabet was invented by Sequoya, a member of the only tribe to have its own written language and newspaper. A hasty polling of my classes revealed that students knew Sequoya as the name of the U.S. President's refurbished yacht on the Potomac River.

In 1990, I received a grant to study Literary Profiles of Native American Women. That summer was memorable. For six weeks, I visited the Library of Congress each day and examined lifestyles of Native American women as depicted in literature.

Because of that project, I came to believe in the uniqueness, strength, and dignity of Native American women, especially those who are literally caught between two cultures. They must keep their own identities while being economically forced to be mainstreamed into our white culture. Many find success in arts and crafts, where they can express their heritage and project their tribal identities at the same time they adapt to changing Twenty-first Century lifestyles and reconcile their native spirituality with organized religion.

Few people realize that for the most part, Native American women determined who sat in tribal councils, and they chose the war chiefs, a process that wielded considerable political power. Their advice was often asked for in tribal council, and they could vote.

In some cases, they were the equals of male warriors, and many Indian women were as famous in war as they were in council. In other cases, men were often absent in battle or hunting so the tribes relied on women to maintain stability in community life. Most women accepted this, and some even relished their role as providers. Generally, there was a blending of male and female roles because harmony and mutual respect were the primary objectives.

So, because of that grant, I gained an appreciation for Native American women that I never had when I went to high school. All I had was that statute of Owatonna in my hometown park, and I found there was so much more to the Native American woman than that.

Like a colorful Indian blanket, common threads were woven throughout the literary works that I introduced to my students: the negative effects of individuality and personal success; the connectedness with all who share this planet; the propriety of kinship; the power of figurative language, symbols, songs, and stories; and the rich and long literary heritage of Native American women adventurers who had to adapt to the demands of the modern world.

Admittedly, most tribes acknowledged women's vital role in the creative process--she was portrayed as the giver of life and a cohesive life force. Some tribes believed she had mystical power over the life cycle.

The concept that a woman was made from man is not found in Native American religion. Females are created simultaneously with males, and each is endowed with peculiar qualities and sensibilities and is dependent upon the other for existence. Neither is accorded supremacy. Most tribes are matrilineal; that is, they pass both clan names and ownership of property through the females.

Consequently, the works I read with my students were peopled with women finding their identities and women confronting religious conviction and quandaries. Their dreams, devotions and desires were no different from mine and those of my students. We found that there was a universality of emotion and intellect existing under the minority label of "Indian" because all women embrace the Iroquois Great Law of Peace:

The chain of culture is the chain of women
linking the past with the future.

But it was the power of the word and the Indians' reverence for symbols, songs, and stories in the form of folktales, autobiographies and imaginative narratives that became most precious to me as an English teacher.

"In the beginning was the word," so for the Native Americans, communing with the forces of nature and with each other about work, love, death, fear, and the past is important. Indian writer Leslie Marmon Silko said, "You don't have anything if you don't have the stories."

Another Indian writer of the Kiowa tribe, N. Scott Momaday, wrote, "The possibilities of storytelling are precisely those of understanding human experience." In this time of flashy images flickering across a television or video screen, what a joy it is to find a group holding on to its stories and realizing the value of oral communication—people talking to people, much like the purpose of the *Minnesota Memories* series.

The finest anthology that I found was published by the Minnesota Humanities Commission, *Braided Lives: An Anthology of Multicultural American Writing* (1991), and in that collection, there was no other work that so moved students to respond, discuss Native American stereotypes, and recollect their own experiences with Native Americans than Diane Burns' poem, "Sure You Can Ask Me A Personal Question," pp. 65-66.

Sure You Can Ask Me a Personal Question
by Diane Burns

How do you do?
No, I am not Chinese
No, not Spanish.
No, I am American Indi—uhh, Native American.
No, not from India.
No, not Apache.
No, not Navajo.
No, not Sioux.
No, we are not extinct.
Yes, Indian.
Oh? So that's where you got those high cheekbones.
Your great grandmother, huh?
An Indian Princess, huh?
Hair down to there?
Let me guess, Cherokee?
Oh, so you've had an Indian friend?
That close?
Oh, so you've had an Indian lover?
That tight?
Oh, so you've had an Indian servant?
That much?
Yeah, it was awful what you guys did to us.
It's real decent of you to apologize.
No, I don't know where you can get peyote.
No, I don't know where you can get Navajo rugs real cheap.
No, I didn't make this. I bought it at Bloomingdale's.
Thank you, I like your hair too.
I don't know if anyone knows whether or not Cher is really Indian.
No, I didn't make it rain tonight.
Yeah. Uh-huh. Spirituality.
Uh-huh. Yeah. Spirituality. Uh-huh. Mother Earth.
Yeah. Uh-huh. Uh-huh. Spirituality.
No, I didn't major in archery.
Yeah, a lot of us drink too much.
Some of us can't drink enough. This ain't no stoic look.

One year, my class even won a grant to build a Native American courtyard, and we planted native grasses, trees and shrubs. We began a Native American Storytelling Club in the elementary grades. Students met in our courtyard's tepee once a week to learn about Native American plants, family life and medicine. They read legends, completed crafts projects, and convened a Story-Telling Festival for parents, teachers, siblings, and the community.

The club not only raised awareness of the Indian population in their suburban neighborhood but also focused attention on the art of storytelling in a fun and educational way. I also took my students to the Smithsonian to view the collected paintings of George Catlin. I began to collect artifacts that I could display and embellish my teaching units with. Later, these artifacts became part of my home's décor after I researched my findings: a caribou doll and ivory carvings from the Aleuts, Tlingit masks from the Northwest, a painted drum from a Cheyenne artist, some Ojibwa bead work, a Hopi woven rug, shell beads from the Seminoles, and a Sioux buffalo robe.

My proudest possession was a mounted buffalo head which I used to drag into class so students could appreciate the Indian's use of the American bison: the hooves that became water vessels; the horns that became scoops, spoons, powder horns, hot coal carriers, and ornaments; the skull itself which became a ceremonial tool; the tongue which was food; the brains which were used for tanning hides; the fat and tallow, which was used for cooking oil, ointment, grease for waterproofing and hair dressing; and the hide itself, which served so many uses.

My collection is small. Many were purchased from the Indian gift shop at the Department of Interior in Washington and on my travels throughout the country or from Native American craftspeople at pow-wows, but I enjoy each piece, and upon my death, I will donate most to a small Nanticoke Indian Museum outside Bethany Beach, Delaware.

I also traveled to points of interest that embellished my class's readings: the site of Wounded Knee (1890), a trip to view the white albino buffalo on my way to Bismarck, North Dakota, a visit to the Mandan mound village outside Ft. Abraham Lincoln in North Dakota, and a drive to the Effigy Mounds National Monument near the Mississippi River.

This summer, I plan to visit Crazy Horse's Monument, the giant mountain sculpture begun by Korczak Ziolkowski which will become the largest statue in the world. The nine-story-high face of Crazy Horse is not complete, but I can see ongoing work on this memorial at the same time that I visit the museum and educational and cultural center there.

I particularly enjoyed sharing my small collection of Native American jewelry with my classes, and we talked of the animal and circle motifs found on many pieces. Most did not know that the art of Indian jewelry making did not begin until 1850 and that the first Navajo silver jewelry was made from American silver dollars. That practice continued until 1890, when the U.S. government enforced a law forbidding the use of money for making jewelry.

The year when the Chandler-Pohrt Collection of Woodland and Plains Indian clothing was exhibited at the Smithsonian in Washington, D.C., I took my classes to view the designs of porcupine quill embroidery and bead work. The artifacts dated from 1780 to 1920, and our students from the fashion merchandising classes especially appreciated the craftsmanship.

Last January on the same evening that President Bush held his State of the Union address only a block away in the U.S. Capital, Wilma Mankiller of Oklahoma lectured to a standing-room audience in the National Museum of the American Indian's auditorium. She began by telling us of her experience checking into a hotel that day. When she signed the roster as "Wilma Mankiller," the clerk asked if that was her real name. She replied in the affirmative and was immediately surrounded by Secret Service agents, unaware that this powerful lady was no threat to any Head of State but was the personification of courage and a dispenser of wisdom, a Native American Head of State, a chief of the Cherokee Nation. No wonder we stood and offered her a standing ovation. She brought humor and insight to an audience that knew of her devotion and dedication to all Native Americans and women everywhere.

So, Owatonna, you are more than my hometown. Your city seal depicts Princess Owatonna with her arms raised to honor the incomparable landscape of Mineral Springs Park, a time gone forever, and the formidable accomplishments of Native American Women everywhere.

Never again will I underestimate the impact of a city, a myth, and a name on an inhabitant's psyche, lifestyle, interests, hobbies and identity. Princess Owatonna's spirit has endured and found its way into my home furnishings, my hobby of collecting Native American artifacts, my travel choices, my reading selections, and most importantly, my teaching of Native American literary selections. Owatonna has been and always will be truly a part of me.

Princess Owatonna

Mother of the Civil Rights Movement
by Jeanetta M. Richardson

I was a 7-year-old Minneapolis girl visiting my Michigan grandparents for the summer as I had done for the previous couple of years. My grandfather, a pastor, was often invited to attend other churches' conventions and on occasion give a sermon as a guest at other churches. This visit to Michigan would not be like any other because who I would meet would have an influence in my life as I grew older. The person I met was Rosa Parks, and she was attending St. Matthew's A.M.E. Church. I had the privilege to meet and sit with her.

I knew little about how her refusing to give up her seat on an Alabama bus helped to shape the history of African American people in their fight to achieve civil rights. Not knowing who she was might have been a good thing because I was not intimidated. We were introduced by my grandmother, and I sat with Rosa for the service. She signed my program, and I still have it tucked away in my trunk. Every once in awhile, as I go through life here in Minnesota, I take out that program and reflect on my experience.

Since I was only 7, I don't remember what we talked about. What I do remember and what amazes me now is how approachable, humble and friendly she was. Here was an African American woman who made history one day in 1955, attending church and praying with all us average people. As I grew up, I read and watched television accounts about important civil rights leaders like Malcolm X, Martin Luther King, and ordinary people of all backgrounds who were trying to make a difference in this country, and Rosa Parks was always mentioned.

Being a woman and a person of color, Rosa Parks still inspires me to stand up for myself, but also for those who are not able to speak up for themselves and do for themselves. Much work still needs to be done to achieve equality for all people through nonviolent means. We must watch, listen and reflect on these issues, talk about and bring awareness whenever we can.

I was saddened to hear of Rosa Parks' passing in 2005, for we all have lost a great leader and role model. Her physical presence may be gone, but her spirit lives in all of us who met her, heard stories told by the previous generation, or read about her in history books. Rosa Parks will continue to make history long after her passing, for I will continue to tell her story and live the legacy she has left for all Americans who struggle for equality.

Rosa Parks

Jeanetta M. Richardson is a student at Metropolitan State University in Saint Paul, pursuing an individualized B.A. degree in International Relations. She is 27 years old and lives in Brooklyn Park.

On the Stupidity of Turkeys
by Tom Veblen

As a boy in Hallock, I was somewhat of an entrepreneur, always trying new ventures to earn money so I could buy the things I wanted and thought I needed. One year I decided to earn money by raising turkeys. I'd been told that turkeys were hard to raise but were highly profitable. High risks with big rewards--my kind of game. The year before I'd had a very hard time coming to grips with having to slaughter the chickens I raised, but through that experience, I had learned and matured. After the chicken fiasco, I had things to prove. Having made the jump to chicken killer, how tough could it be to slaughter turkeys?

I rented an unused coop that belonged to our block-away neighbors, the Bergs, ordered 106 turkey poults, and steeled myself for the next round of poultry venturing.

And so it happened that early one late spring morning I rose before dawn to meet the Great Northern two-car mail train that Hallock folks affectionately called "the dinky" so I could retrieve my shipment of furiously peeping birds. The train arrived, and I brought home two boxes of 3-day old turkey poults.

Unfortunately, I didn't fully understand just how seriously dumb turkeys really are. For instance, they're so dumb that they will stand in a heavy rainstorm with their heads raised and their beaks open and drown. They are so dumb that, as one wag put it, "If they threw themselves at the ground, they'd miss." They are so dumb that in a thunderstorm they will stampede into a corner and smother themselves to death. And that's exactly what mine did.

One spring afternoon, three weeks into the venture, I was in school. Absorbed in my studies, I failed to notice the low muttering of a thunderstorm as it slowly came rolling in from the north. Then, with a sudden squall of rain, a flash of lightning, and a sharp clap of thunder, the storm was upon us. The wind-driven rain moving along the front of the storm rattled on the windows and cut off all visibility to the north. "Oh my God," I thought, "my birds!"

It was three quarters of a mile to the coop, straight into the approaching storm. I shot out the classroom door, down the hall, out the side door, out across the play yard, and out across the vacant lot next to where the Wickies lived.

By the time I reached the coop, I was soaking wet and winded. Opening the door and peering into the gloom, I could see two or three turkey poults standing forlornly in the middle of the room, peeping dishearteddly while pecking dispiritedly at the wood shavings that covered the floor.

As my eyes adjusted, I could just discern, in the southwest corner of the room, a pile of feathers. My flock, spooked by the thunder, had piled into the corner and there smothered themselves. Talk about seriously dumb! So much for my new bike, skates, and gun.

And so much, for the time being, for entrepreneurship.

Hallock native Tom Veblen is a retired general management consultant living in Washington, D.C. with his wife Linda. He has five adult children and enjoys writing. His book, "The Way of Business: An Inquiry into Meaning and Superiority" is available at www.kamprint.com/pcurrent.html or SuperbizRT@aol.com.

Billy and the Rope
by Alice Stielow

There were seven of us Nilson kids on a farm near Clinton, and we all had our own special quirks. Billy is the brother who was always into something. It made no difference what we did to keep him contained in the yard, he always got out and would wander away.

The folks put up a fence around the yard, thinking that would solve the problem, but being fenced in was not for him. He just crawled over and was off to explore. The thing was, he was such a little mite it was hard to spot him, and as small as his legs were, they could dash off so quickly it took an army to keep up with him.

He followed in Daddy's footsteps. Wherever Daddy was, Billy was sure to follow. One day he followed Daddy to the barn, through the lean-to, and out the door, where he fell into a big hog wallow. A wallow is a mud puddle the pigs lie in during the summer time to keep cool. Pigs have no sweat glands so they like to lie in the mud to keep cool.

Well there Billy was--stuck fast. This time his little legs just wouldn't get him out. He was screaming so loudly that he chased all the pigs out of the wallow, and in their hurry to get away from that terrible noise coming out of that little kid, they spattered him with mud from head to the waist, and anything below his waist was already stuck fast in the muck and mud.

Daddy didn't hear him yelling, but I happened to be close by and came to his rescue. Sometimes I think I should have left him there for awhile so he would have learned a lesson. But no, I laid a board on the mud hoping it would hold me until I could reach the little menace. Well, it did a good job of holding me until I lifted him, and then the weight was too much for the board.

Not only Billy, but I also was knee deep in muck and mud. Now believe me, I didn't like wallowing in the mud right then because it wasn't just mud--it was pig poopy mud.

I finally got him out and took him to the house, thinking someone would feel sorry for me and clean the kid up. Oh no, Mother brought a pail or water outside, and it was there that he got a scrubbing that was good enough so I could get him in the bathtub without dripping mud and pig poop all over the kitchen. Now, he doesn't think to this day he ever did anything wrong, but I tell you he did.

We had a salesman who came to the farm selling Raleigh products, His name was Howard Vogel, and he was interesting to talk to. One day he came into the yard about the time we were all running around looking for the little menace again.

Mr Vogel joined the search for Billy because he had run away one time when he was a little boy, and he had gone to the grain field, where his father was cutting grain with a binder. He told us that as his father approached him, he stuck up his arm and hollered to his dad, but it was too late. His father cut off his arm with the binder. Because of this accident, Mr. Vogel was always concerned when a kid was missing, even for a short time.

We hadn't even thought of looking in the field, and Daddy was out north of the trees cutting grain. Off we went as fast as our legs could carry us, and there we saw a little blond towhead above the grain. I shudder to think what could have happened had Mr. Vogel not come that day.

We couldn't understand why Billy was always running off. It wasn't like he didn't have things to do close to the house. My folks had made a sand pile, he had little trucks and trailers to play with, and he also had a tricycle that he could ride up and down the sidewalk. There were huge elm trees that shaded the sand pile and sidewalk. It was a perfect place for a little boy to entertain himself.

That night there was a long conversation in our house as to how we could keep track of Billy. Mr. Vogel had said Mother should make a halter for him and tie him up when he was outside. Boy, that sounded almost too cruel, but that is just what happened. Mother made the halter so it buttoned in the back, and Billy couldn't get it off. Try as he might, he just couldn't get it off.

Then came the rope. Boy, if you ever saw an angry little boy, it was the first time Mother tied Billy to the fence. He screamed and screamed. Well, at least we could hear him and knew where he was. It took several days until the screaming stopped and he decided he could really play there. He tells me he remembers being tied up too.

It is with glee that I remember him being tied to the fence, thus giving the rest of us a little peace of mind. The rest of that summer was a little more peaceful for everyone, and we always remembered the nice man who gave Mother the idea that it wasn't cruel to tie him up for safety sake. He wished his mother had done that to him those many years ago. Yes, Billy was a handful, and I think it followed him to this day.

Billy Nilson

Alice Stielow and her husband Richard have lived on the same farm near Clinton for nearly forty years. They have five daughters, one son, twenty-two grandchildren and thirty-one great grandchildren.

The 1941 Telephone Caper
by Anastasia "Stacy" Vellas

It was a glorious day, perfect for an adventure. My brother Connie and I set out on the trail to the boat landing at the spring on the south side of Third Guide Lake. The sun was still high in the afternoon sky. I placed one foot in front of the other in a run walk beside my brother on the trail along the fence at the north side of the garden and on up the hill.

Northern Minnesota is a land of many hills. At the top of the first rise, nestled in tall grass just above the garden, was a small family cemetery. We stopped and looked in at the hollows where my grandmother and her two children were buried. Leon had died of diphtheria when he was 4, and Cora Lucille had died of pneumonia at age 6. Grandmother had leakage of the heart, I was told.

I often stopped by this quiet, pleasant cemetery and visited my grandmother. She died two years before I was born so I never knew her, but my mother talked about her often. Looking back, I can't remember ever seeing Mama visit the graves in all the years we lived on the homestead. She often discussed her family with me however, so I knew everything about each person.

The fence around the graves had no gate, and we never went in. I picked a small blossom from the wild roses that grew along the fence. Connie yelled, "Let's go, Stacy!" I turned back toward the trail and continued on up the hill where he waited.

The dandelions were in bloom with their little yellow faces turned to greet the sun and me as I passed by. I picked one, put it under my chin and asked Connie, "Do I like butter?"

Of course, the bright golden bloom beneath my chin reflected the dandelion's yellow glow. "Yes, you like butter," he told me.

Daddy had a log house built on Grandpa's homestead when we moved there in 1932, the year after my brother Connie was born. We had a hundred and sixty acres to explore. We had to hoe weeds in the strawberry patch in the spring, and we had to chop and bring in wood and do a few other chores. But if we didn't have any work, we would take off into the woods without asking permission. Mama never paid much attention to us. She was always busy with her duties. Out of earshot, we could always say, "We didn't hear you call."

It was too early to go home and wait for supper. "Connie," I said, "let's take the boat out and row over to O'Brien's place and see what they left when they moved."

"Okay," he said. Before the O'Brien family moved to Shovel Lake, we used to row the boat across the lake and visit the kids. Charley O'Brien was about my age. Loretta O'Brien was older and so pretty. The O'Brien kids went to Shovel Lake School. We were in Aitkin County, and we went to the Swatara School. We hadn't seen the O'Brien kids since they moved.

The long days of summer gave us plenty of daylight as we followed the trail to the crest of the hill. The grass grew high along the trail as a result of frequent rains. Wood ticks were not as bad now as they were in the early spring. Before we entered the wooded area we usually stopped and picked the ticks off. Breaking off a small branch from a poplar tree, we swung the branch back and forth around our body to keep the mosquitoes away as we continued through the woods to the spring.

The trail along the crest of the hill was on level ground. Tall poplar trees and the few pines shaded us from the sun. After about a quarter of a mile, the trail made a right turn and dropped down a sharp incline that brought us abruptly to the spring on the shore of Third Guide Lake.

The boat was tied up at the spring where Daddy had left it the last time he had gone fishing. Climbing over fallen limbs, I jumped into the boat and put the oars in the oarlocks ready to row the boat across the lake. Connie picked up the anchor, put it in the boat, and pushed the boat out in the water. He climbed in and began bailing water that had seeped in since the last time the boat was used.

I began rowing the boat across the lake. The stretch and pull with the oars was easy for a strong girl of 13. It was only about half a mile across the lake. After awhile Connie took his turn at the oars and guided the boat to O'Brien's landing.

In the early days, before 1900, surveyors running lines on the land named the lake Third Guide. They found they had to make an adjustment in their measurements because two-thirds of the lake was in Aitkin County, and the guideline at the Cass County line was short by one-third. The lake was on the third guideline.

A warm breeze came up as we pulled the boat partly out of the water at O'Brien's landing and dropped the anchor to make sure the boat wouldn't drift off. If it did we would have a long walk home around the north side of the lake.

We took the old wagon road through the pines that led to the O'Brien house. The grass was tall but the ruts were still visible. The O'Briens had moved to Shovel Lake about a year ago, and their garden was overgrown with weeds. Old rusty machinery leaned against the small out buildings. A rabbit scurried across our path startling both of us.

We soon came upon the out buildings. It was very quiet here. A squirrel shimmied up a tree and looked down at us. The whine of the wind in the pines made it all the scarier. We tugged on the door of the first shed, and I jumped back when the door creaked. Cautiously we looked inside the building hoping to find some small treasure they had left behind. All was quiet. There was only the wind.

We continued on to the house, a short distance away. At every little noise we stopped and listened, ready to turn and run. The house had a high peaked roof and was surrounded by tall pines. The house still had a few small patches of paint. I knocked just to be safe. No answer. I turned the doorknob and gave a push. I gave a harder push. Connie helped push, and the door gave and came open with a loud creak. We jumped back and listened. Was there someone there? I called out, "Hello, anybody home?" No one answered.

Connie spoke up, “There’s nobody here. They moved, I told you. One of the kids said they moved to Shovel Lake. I heard it at school.” After a pause we went in. Carefully inching our way, we crossed the room. I looked around. The quiet was frightening.

The wooden floors were dusty. Spider webs splayed across the ceiling and in the corners by the windows. We left tracks in the dust as we walked from room to room. It had been a long time since anyone had been here. The next room appeared to be the kitchen with a pantry off to the side. They left nothing but scraps of paper.

Even though we found nothing, it was still exciting to explore the inside of the house. It was so different from our house, which was just one big room. Our floors had wide boards with cracks between. We seldom visited other people. Sometimes we visited my mother’s sister, Aunt Elsie. She had a nice house, but her house was always cluttered, and Mama began cleaning as soon as she got there.

Now here we were in the O’Briens’ house. Although it was empty, it was still exciting. We wandered through the rooms and looked out the windows at the tall pine trees that shaded the house. At every strange sound, I grabbed Connie’s arm. “Are you scared?”

“No,” Connie said, “There’s nobody here. Girls are always scared.” Nevertheless, he jumped when a tree limb banged against the house.

Finally, we came to a door that went into the living room. There was no furniture in there either. There was just a door opening out onto the front porch and the door we had just entered. But there was something in the room. I saw it first. “Connie, Look! A telephone!” He looked and gasped. He was as excited as I was.

I remember Mama telling me that in the early days everyone who had a telephone had many parties on one line. You could take the receiver off and listen to people’s conversations. In 1941, you had to turn the crank to contact Central, and Central would ring your party.

There it was on the wall, a large wooden telephone with a hand crank to call Central. We turned the crank and tried several times to call Central, but there was no answer. We tried to yell into the round metal mouthpiece, but it was no use. The phone was dead.

I knew when I saw that telephone that I had to have it. Connie would go along because I knew he wanted it too. Few people ventured out onto the back roads in the north woods. Many old houses stood vacant after homesteaders grew too old to farm or moved into town. Sometimes during hunting season a hunter would come by. The O'Brien house was at the end of a long dirt road that branched off the main road to Shovel Lake. No one lived out this far anymore. Still we listened outside to be sure no car would arrive unannounced.

I wasn't worried about it being wrong. The only thing that concerned me was how to sneak the phone to our place without my parents catching us. Would anyone expect two kids to walk several miles and remove a telephone from a vacant house? I didn't reason it out or worry. I just saw something I wanted, and it was mine for the taking.

"I want that telephone, Connie," I told him. He was usually willing to do anything I wanted to do.

"Okay, if we can get it off the wall." We tugged on it, we shook it hard, but it was clamped there pretty tight. We tugged some more and we pulled and pulled. Finally it came off the wall and landed with a bang on the floor. Oh, it was a heavy thing, solid oak, I'm sure.

After we got it down, we still had to carry it at least half a mile back to the boat. It was so heavy. Could we get it back to the boat by ourselves? I was 13 and long-legged, but very skinny. Connie was small. He had just turned 10 in February.

We started back down the wagon road toward the boat. I took the heavy end, and Connie took the light end, and we held it waist high. Turned sideways to each other we carried it between us down the road. Wouldn't you know it? Connie tripped and the phone fell to the ground.

We turned it over and looked to see if there was any damage, and it seemed to be all right. After resting a few minutes, we lifted it and started toward the boat. We only went a short way before we had to stop and rest again. We finally reached the boat and laid it on the board that served as a back seat.

Connie held the telephone against the seat with both hands so it wouldn't fall off into the water that had seeped into the boat, and I rowed the boat across the lake. We knew if it got wet it wouldn't be any good.

Determined to take that telephone home, we also were determined not to get caught. We never thought beyond that. We didn't even have telephone lines!

By the time we reached the spring, it was getting late in the afternoon, and we were getting kind of scared and didn't want to get caught. We knew supper would be ready soon so we'd better get home. Connie said, "We need to hide the phone and come back for it later." I agreed, and we started looking for a safe place.

I said, "Aren't there some little islands over by the east shore?"

"Yes," Connie said, "Let's find a dry one."

I rowed the boat to the east side of the lake where the creek entered Third Guide. We pulled up to one of the islands, and Connie checked the mounds for dampness. He found a dry island and with both of us holding the telephone, we eased it out of the boat and laid it on dry grass. We turned the boat and headed for the landing. At the spring we pulled the boat out of the water. Taking the trail back to the house, we made plans to come back for the telephone, take it to our place and hide it in the woods. That wouldn't be hard to do because no one ever checked on us kids.

Supper was almost ready when we got home. Mama had cooked a venison roast. She mashed the boiled potatoes, made gravy and opened a jar of vegetables. She had even managed to make my favorite chocolate bread pudding for dessert. She asked me to beat the whipping cream with the eggbeater until it stood up in peaks.

As we sat down at the table and ate, Daddy and Mama began talking and did not notice that Connie and I were quiet. No one had missed us. No one asked where we had been.

That spring Daddy had moved the family from the homestead into the green schoolhouse a little more than two miles from the farm. The schoolhouse was next to the county road that went to Outing, with telephone lines just a couple hundred feet from the house.

We waited a few days before we went to get the phone. We took the rowboat out again, picked up the phone, and together carried it to the green schoolhouse. Connie hid the phone in his playhouse in the woods. When Mama and Daddy went to town, he took it over by the chicken coop, where two wires were hanging from the telephone line next to the road. He hooked it up to the wires, but he couldn't get any response. Then he put it back in his playhouse.

Connie told me, "I took the telephone apart, and inside there was a magnet. I found that when you cranked, it produced electricity. It had enough electricity to ring the bell at Central, and Central would plug in to the switchboard and ring the number. I also learned that when you cranked the handle it made a spark. I found that out after getting shocked.

"I got some tools and took the little cranking mechanism out. I was going to put the telephone wire under the sheet in the bed where my sisters slept and give them a shock, but I never got around to it. I even put it in the water to get the fish shocked. But that didn't work. A boy in school told me that if you put an electric wire in water and turned the crank it would electrocute the fish, and you could go out and scoop them up. Well, I tried it and it didn't work."

I never told anyone we stole a telephone, and I never did get to use that telephone. I waited for Connie to hook it up, but it never happened. I can only say that for a little while I owned a crank telephone. Now I have my own telephone, and it has always been a delight to me. Ma Bell shut off my four-party 8709-J-4 number when they took out the party lines and forced this new number on me. . . Call me anytime at 760-344-4494. If I'm not here, leave a message and I'll get back to you!

Third Guide Lake
by Stacy Vellas

Along the third meridian
Where Cass and Aitkin Counties divide
The surveyors made an adjustment
And they called the lake "Third Guide."

In this land of tall white pine
George Harrington took out a claim
When the land was in its prime
And the forests teemed with game.

Blueberries grew on the north hill
Cranberries filled the wet bogs
There was farm land if you had the will
And trees to cut for logs.

Along tote roads of yesterday
The earth grew and gave its all
Wild rice grew in the bay
That Indians gathered in fall

Today, you can put in a boat at
Harrington's Dam for George's sake
And row on up Moose River
Until you come to Third Guide Lake

Anastasia "Stacy" Vellas moved from Swatara to California in 1944. After working as a waitress and field worker, she became a teacher. The mother of five sons, she lives in Brawly, California.

About Minnesota Memories 6

I have always considered myself a Minnesotan. While living in other states, I enjoyed getting together with fellow Minnesotans to share stories about life in the North Star State. These stories not only entertained, but they refreshed and restored whatever it was about my mind and soul that needed refreshment and restoration.

In 2000, I was teaching in Maryland, and across the hall was another native Minnesotan, Kathy Megyeri. One day, after Kathy sold a story to the *Chicken Soup* publishers, I said, "Somebody should compile a book of stories about life in Minnesota. Every Minnesotan has at least one good, true story or recollection, and a compilation of all those stories would make a terrific book." We pitched that idea to a few publishers of regional books, and they pitched it right back.

After recovering from this rejection, we decided that we would take it upon ourselves to compile and publish a book of extraordinary stories by ordinary Minnesota folks. When we contacted old friends, only a few responded and sent stories because many doubted that we would actually publish a book. Undaunted, we confounded those skeptics, wrote some of our own stories, combined them with a few we received from other people, and published *Minnesota Memories* in 2001.

I traveled more than 10,000 miles that first summer, from Grand Marais to Austin and from Adrian to Winona--talking to newspaper reporters and radio interviewers about my *Minnesota Memories* mission. I spoke at county fairs, schools, class reunions, book stores, trade shows, service clubs, church groups and historical societies, inviting ordinary people to send their extraordinary stories for *Minnesota Memories 2*.

The response was terrific. Since that time, I have traveled thousands of additional miles meeting people all over Minnesota, collecting and publishing hundreds of their stories in six volumes. This is so much fun that I intend to keep publishing *Minnesota Memories* books until all the great Minnesota stories have been preserved in print--or until I conk out, whichever comes first.

Joan Claire Graham, Purveyor of Memories

Do you have a true story to submit for *Minnesota Memories 7?*

Send your true stories for the next volume.

Minnesota Memories
439 Lakeview Boulevard
Albert Lea, Minnesota 56007
or email them to MinnMemory@aol.com.

To book a program for your organization, library, store, historical society, writers' group, or school call 507-377-1255.

Back of the Book Special!

If you made it all the way to the last paragraph of the last page, you deserve a break. Order any book from the *Minnesota Memories* series for $12. Minnesota residents add 78 cents sales tax. I will pay the postage. For a complete 6-volume set of *Minnesota Memories* books, send $68. Minnesota residents add $4.40 tax, and I will still pay the postage. Make checks to *Minnesota Memories*.

What a great gift this would make!

Writers from these towns submitted stories for *Minnesota Memories 6*. Is there a story from your town?